UNSCRAMBLING SPELLING

Cynthia Klein and Robin R. Millar

UNSCRAMBLING SPELLING

Cynthia Klein & Robin R. Millar

Hodder & Stoughton

A MEMBER OF THE HODDER HEADLINE GROUP

Acknowledgments

We wish to thank our colleagues at the Language and Literacy Unit and the many tutors and teachers throughout ILEA who have given us their unending support and inspiration in stimulating ideas and materials. We are also grateful to the many patient and persevering students who have taught us as much about learning as we have taught them.

We would like to dedicate this book to the memory of Aisling O'Reilly Barnett, a gifted teacher and much loved colleague and friend.

The publishers would like to thank the following for permission to reproduce material in this volume:

B. T. Batsford Ltd for material from *The Skills of Handwriting* by R. C. Phillips (1976); Tony Buzan for the diagram from *Use Your Head* New Revised Edition, BBC Publications (1989); Gabriel Systems for the extract from *The Gregorc Delineator Systems*; Holt, Rinehart and Winston for the diagram from *Comprehension and Learning* by F. Smith (1975); Margaret Peters for the activity from *Success In Spelling*, Cambridge Institute of Education (1970) and for the dictation passage from *Diagnostic and Remedial Spelling* Manual, Macmillan Education (1975).

Every effort has been made to trace and acknowledge ownership of copyright. The publishers would be happy to make suitable arrangements with those copyright holders whom it has not been possible to contact.

Orders: please contact Bookpoint Ltd, 130 Milton Park, Abingdon, Oxon OX14 4SB. Telephone: (44) 01235 827720, Fax: (44) 01235 400454. Lines are open from 9.00 - 6.00, Monday to Saturday, with a 24 hour message answering service. Email address: orders@bookpoint.co.uk

British Library Cataloguing in Publication Data
A catalogue record for this title is available from The British Library

ISBN 0-340-51234-2

First Published 1990
Impression number   16
Year   2004 2003 2002

Typeset by Taurus Graphics, Abingdon, Oxon
Printed in Great Britain for Hodder & Stoughton Educational, a division of Hodder Headline Plc, 338 Euston Road, London NW1 3BH
Printed by Hobbs the Printers, Southampton.

Contents

Introduction

It seems that spelling has always been an educational issue, with fierce proponents of the view that 'You're not educated unless you spell correctly' and equally staunch supporters of the 'Spelling doesn't matter, it's the content that counts' school.

We believe that learning to spell can give students greater confidence and willingness to develop their writing skills. Many of the students with whom we have worked are those who 'failed' at spelling in school. Few of them were taught spelling and most never 'caught' the skill. Our aim is to encourage teachers to *teach* spelling, through using students' own written words as the basis of an individualised spelling programme. We explain how teachers can, together with students, analyse these words, develop an individual scheme for each student and discover effective strategies for remembering spellings. We also offer suggestions as to how such an individualised approach can be integrated into the classroom.

Included in this book are photocopiable resource sheets which may be used to stimulate discussion about spelling, learning and language issues. However, we would also encourage teachers to extend these and develop their own which may be more relevant to their particular class or group. We find that by acquiring a better understanding of words, word constructions and their own learning strategies, students become more interested in and enthusiastic about language work. We hope that work on spelling may facilitate language development and provide a base for continuing student progress.

Although we hope that some teachers may find it useful to follow the spelling programme as we have presented it, we also intend this book as a resource and reference guide that teachers may dip into in order to explore particular topics, to find suggestions for specific students and to stimulate interest and wonder in words.

SECTION 1: INTRODUCING SPELLING

Why Teach Spelling?

Students and teachers alike often feel that working on spelling is a necessary evil. They find spelling manuals and books boring and ineffective in helping students to improve their spelling. Hours may be spent filling out spelling workbooks only to find that the student still makes spelling errors in his or her writing.

Many students may have experienced previous spelling lessons as instant and constant failure. Not only did they regularly get seven out of ten wrong, but teachers reacted to their failure as a character deficiency, giving the impression that good spelling was seen to be an example of superior moral fibre rather than a useful skill.

On the other hand, there may be many students who never had any spelling instruction at all! They muddle along, hoping that their own spelling strategies might work, no matter how ineffective or inefficient these strategies are. 'They used to tell me to go away and learn the spellings, but nobody ever told me *how*' is a common cry from students with spelling problems. Some students are left with an inability to read back their own writing and no method to learn how to spell.

There are many misconceptions about the nature of spelling and its value in writing, as well as uncertainties about effective memorisation methods for learning new words. All of this has given spelling a bad name. Students *can* learn to spell and benefit from this tuition. An organised and serious programme of spelling can offer a number of benefits to *any* student, even those with crippling spelling problems. The results are of great value and well worth the time and energy.

What are the benefits?

(See Resource Sheet 1.)

1 Spelling improves

In some cases, specific spelling difficulties may not disappear, but the actual spelling *performance* will improve. This means students will consistently be able to write many words correctly which were not previously in their spelling vocabulary. Many writing tasks, from shopping lists to essays, can be undertaken with accuracy and confidence. Students can begin to

say, 'I know how to spell that word' instead of 'I'm not sure I know that.'

2 Self-confidence improves

Because spellings can be and are learned, students' confidence in themselves as writers will improve. There will be benefits for the students both in performance and self-esteem. They will have actual proof that they *can* learn. As one student said, 'I can look back and see all the spellings I now know that I didn't know six months ago.'

Not surprisingly, this positive learning experience can generate success in other learning situations. The student can see that if spellings can be learned, so can other topics or material and they gain the confidence to tackle academic work which may formerly have intimidated them.

3 Spelling errors that do remain will be more readable

Many students (and sometimes teachers) find it difficult to distinguish a 'good' spelling mistake (or one that shows an understanding of English spelling convention) from a 'bad' (or disordered) spelling. By devoting time to learning words, students will learn about the consistencies of English letter patterns and thus begin to make more 'logical' errors. This knowledge will reduce the severity of spelling problems for many students. In turn, students will feel empowered by understanding the nature of their errors and will feel more in control of their mistakes and their learning.

For some students, spelling may never be perfect. However, by working on spelling they will learn more conventional (or readable) spelling possibilities. They may continue to make many errors but the severity of these errors should lessen.

4 Writing fluency improves

Because students now automatically remember more words, they don't have to stop and think about word constructions when writing. Rather than being preoccupied with spelling (remembering words), students can focus their energies on the writing process and getting thoughts down on paper. Writing is faster, more consistent with the thought process, and thus less frustrating and more enjoyable.

5 The quality of writing will improve

Most students with weak spelling (especially those with specific learning difficulties) will have avoided using words they can't spell in their writing. Sentence structure and vocabulary will be over simplified and inappropriate in comparison to the students' verbal abilities or their apparent grasp of the topic. Their inhibited use of language is not because they are intellectually limited, but because the writing must be centred around reproducible spellings.

Once students believe they can learn to spell, they will take greater risks in the use of vocabulary, sentence structure and complexity of topic. Teachers and others who assess their work are more likely to suspend judgement of the spelling if the content seems mature and well thought out.

6 Students will understand the nature of their learning style and needs

Unlike other language skills which are more complex and demanding (such as reading and composing), spelling is a very concise, clear part of language learning. It is dependent on visual-motor memory with rote memorisation playing a large part in the learning process. Because the process of learning to spell is simpler than, for example, learning to read, the errors the student makes can be more thoroughly and easily explained in relation to learning style.

Through analysis of the error, teachers can help students identify their learning style and make recommendations about appropriate learning strategies which suit that style.

7 The English language is demystified

Most weak spellers consider themselves to be 'poor' at English. They feel the language is arbitrarily constructed and inconsistent. Good spelling, they feel,

is inherited (like brown hair) and seems natural to those who are fluent spellers.

By working on their spelling, students will learn more about the structure, derivation and history of the English language. As students gain information and understanding, the mysterious or incomprehensible aspects of language will become less disturbing.

8 Students become better self-critics

Often students feel that a piece of writing containing many errors is 'rubbish'. Like any reader, they are irritated by errors and draw conclusions about the quality of the writing based on the execution of the text. Students may lack the ability to distinguish the difference between content and the technical side of writing.

When students begin to control the medium of spelling, to understand it and to acquire methods of improving it, they become more genuinely able to criticise their writing themselves. Their proofreading skills improve and so does their ability to stand back from a piece of writing and examine it.

9 Students' attention to language will improve

As the process of demystifying English proceeds, students who seemed uninterested in language and language work often change their outlook. They realise that language is challenging rather than impossible. As their understanding increases, their ability to use their learning in other ways is enhanced. For example, we have found that by working on spelling, many students find their decoding, or word attack skills, in reading improve. Other students find their handwriting improves.

Because one aspect of writing gains clarification, students are more willing to look more closely at such things as grammatical structure, the organisation of writing and punctuation without feeling attacked or belittled in the process.

As one student said, 'Since I've been working on my spelling, I've started to find words really interesting – how they're built up, and I use lots of words I never would have thought of using before.'

2

Talking About Spelling

There are many misconceptions and confusions about the nature and/or value of spelling. An important starting point for teachers and students is to discuss the topic. If teachers don't have enough information from students about *how* they learn, they cannot judge whether students are using effective spelling strategies or not. Teachers and students need to share spelling histories and past learning experiences. Myths associated with spelling should be discussed and activities developed which augment these discussions.

Students need to believe in the usefulness of learning to spell, not just because the teacher tells them its a good idea. Teachers can start with some of the activities in this chapter and also Resource Sheet 2. Once students get 'hooked' on spelling, teachers may find they can get quite excited about learning new words.

However, one single discussion about spelling, spelling strategies, language approaches, etc. is not enough. For many students, the discussion needs to take place several times in different contexts, so that the relation of particular language work and spelling is reinforced. Students need to be encouraged to ask questions and *think* about *how* they learn and how they *need* to learn. Current research into adult literacy concludes that the most important skill that teachers can bring to their students is the skill of explaining *why*.

Myths about spelling

We have found that a number of misconceptions and half-truths concerning spelling abound in the minds of students. For good spellers these misconceptions are not particularly distracting; for weak spellers they can be devastating. Teachers often compound these misconceptions by giving misguided advice.

We feel it is important to discuss these half-truths with students so that they can apply their own strategies and methods more easily and adapt them to the realities of learning to spell. Teachers should use the common misunderstandings we list on pp. 3–6 to prompt further discussion with students and clarify which part of the statement is true and which is misleading.

Activity 2.1   Bubbles

Purpose: To begin a discussion with students about the common misconceptions or half-truths concerning the nature and value of spelling.

1 Write each of the 'Myths' listed on pp. 3–6 in large print on a coloured piece of paper or card. Cut these out in 'bubble' shapes.

2 Pin them on the walls around the room. Have students go around in groups and read each one.

3 Break the class into small groups (5–6 per group). Assign each group two or three 'Myths' to discuss. Ask them to identify what's right and wrong about each 'Myth'. Then give students about ten minutes to discuss the 'Myths' in their small groups.

4 Re-group with the whole class and have each group report back their 'findings'. Add comments from the text if students haven't identified all the points.

5 Ask students to:
   (a) Think up other 'Myths' to add to the bubbles.
   (b) Identify which bubbles are the ones they have in the past thought were true.

This activity is reproduced courtesy of Gay Lobley, Director of the Language and Literacy Unit, Southwark College.

Activity 2.2   True/False Spelling Quiz

Purpose: To develop awareness in students of helpful and unhelpful attitudes towards spelling development.

Give the Quiz on Resource Sheet 2 to students. Use the questions as the basis for discussion about confusion in spelling.

'If you want to learn to spell, you should read more.'

Teachers and students alike are confused about the relationship between spelling and reading. It is true that spelling is a sub-skill of writing and that writing is a language skill related to reading. However, as skills, the two activities differ enormously. Much has been written about what happens when we read (see Smith, 1978 and Arnold, 1982).

However, the reading process is both more complex and less demanding than spelling. In reading, we do *not* want to concentrate on the ordering of each letter in a word in order to get meaning from the text. We want to read as efficiently and quickly as possible in order to understand the content of what we read. Reading is dependent on *recognition* skills.

Spelling, on the other hand, is dependent on skills of *recall*. To spell accurately, we must remember all the letters, in sequence. We must pay attention to detail. If we do not, the errors we produce will make it difficult for a reader to decipher our text.

Thus telling students to 'Go away and read more' will help students improve their reading skills but will not necessarily improve their ability to *remember* spellings.

Activity 2.3   Spelling and Reading

Purpose: To show students how we unconsciously apply our knowledge of the probability of certain letter patterns and word derivations when reading.

This activity makes learners aware of some of the benefits of a consistent spelling system. Learners will realise that unconventional spellings will slow down the reader and impede comprehension. They will also be more conscious of the kinds of strategies used in reading an unfamiliar text (for example, reading out loud).

Explain the term 'homonym' to students and give them an example of a complete sentence made up of such words, for instance: 'The none tolled hymn two right two the buoy.' Then carry out the following steps with the class.

1 Divide students into groups. Have each group make up some sentences of the above variety.

2 Collect the sentences from each group.

3 Discuss each sentence and see which aspects make it difficult (or easy) to read.

4 Discuss what reading strategies students might need to decode these sentences.

5 Discuss what problems these kinds of spellings present to the reader. For example, the strain of sounding out each word might put a limit on the reader's ability to remember what he or she has read.

'There's no logic in English spelling – that's why it's so hard.'

Learning to write the English language efficiently and fluently is not an easy task. Learners have many difficulties with English because the spelling of words does not always correspond accurately with the way they are spoken. Some languages correspond exactly to their spoken symbols. Most Romance languages, for example French, Spanish and Italian, are more regular than English.

However, the fact that the English spelling system is not 100 per cent phonetically regular (it is, in fact, 85 per cent regular) does not mean there are no conventions or regularities which can make sense of the spelling system.

Teachers may find that discussing the derviations of language can help readers and writers decipher meaning. Many words in the English language come from other languages and the English spelling is dependent on how that word is spelled (or even pronounced) in the original language.

Activity 2.4   Derivations

Purpose: To show students the development of English vocabulary (and spellings) from foreign words and to give them experience in identifying common (or uncommon) spelling conventions in English.

Introduce this activity with a discussion of the influences of foreign languages on the development of English. Use some of the examples below. (You could also refer to *The Story of English* by Robert McCrum, William Cran and Robert MacNeil for more examples of foreign language influence on English.)

The following words are spelled almost exactly the same in the mother tongue as in English:

Spanish:	llama	'll' at the beginning of a word is not a convention of English
African Bantu:	gnu	'u' at the end of a word is not a convention of English spelling
Hindi:	khaki	'kh' at the beginning of a word is not a convention in English

1 Ask students to refer to dictionaries for this activity.

2 Divide the class into groups. Ask each group to brainstorm about words that they think might be derived from foreign languages.

3 Ask each group to identify *at least* ten different words. These words should be checked in the dictionary for language derivation. (The dictionary can also be used to gather words if necessary.)

4 Each group should make a chart similar to the one above, indicating where each spelling comes from.

5 Gather the lists from all the groups and use for further discussion.

'There is one correct way to learn spellings.'

Many students are embarrassed about the methods they use to learn spellings. They commonly believe that unless you can spell in your head you do not have the 'right' spelling approach. Oral spelling is not only an incredibly demanding and difficult way to spell, but also awkward and unrelated to the circumstances when we ordinarily use spelling – in writing.

One educator has described those people who seem to be born good spellers as 'catchers'. These individuals seem to be able to learn to spell accurately without any (or very little) practice. They have excellent visual memories and can draw on this facility to remember how to spell. But only a small proportion of the people who write are 'catchers'. Many people who are efficient spellers were not born that way. Through identifying their own learning style and fitting strategies to it, students can become successful spellers, even if they're not 'catchers'.

Learners should understand there are *many* effective ways of learning to spell. Their search will be to identify the one that works for them.

Activity 2.5   **Catchers**

Purpose: To show students that most 'good' spellers write down a word to decide whether it is spelled correctly.

1 Ask 'good' spellers in the class or group to identify themselves.

2 Ask them how they decide when a word is correctly spelled. Most students will answer: 'I write it out and then I look at it to see if it is right.'

3 Teachers should make the point that spelling is a *visual* (look at the word) and *motor* (write it out) skill.

'I make spelling mistakes because I don't speak properly.'

A student once commented, 'If I work on my spelling, will I speak like Princes Charles?' This confusion between spoken and written language is a source of bewilderment for many students.

In some ways, because the English spelling system is irregular and compels us to learn words visually (how they look, *not* how they sound), all English language learners are in the same position when learning to spell. No accent or dialect has a particular advantage. For example, people who pronounce 'bath' as 'barth' or 'bahth' will have to visualise the word to eliminate the 'r' or 'h' sound. People who pronounce 'three' as 'tree' will have to visualise the 'h'. Individuals whose accent or dialect omits certain sounds may have a more difficult time learning some of those words.

'If you get stuck, just sound it out.'

English spelling must be learned visually. Sounding out words can be disastrous for students. It is true that we need sounds to help us link into the beginning and/ or structure of words. However, an over-emphasis on sounds will inevitably lead us to discrepancies and word confusions.

Many students, for example, have spent hours learning homonyms, filling in the gaps on worksheets with, for example, 'they're, their and there'. Unfortunately, what they learned was to remember those words in the same chunk. Often students can 'spell' these words correctly, but cannot remember where to use them in the context of their writing. Sounding out the words in these cases will not help.

Students need to learn methods for reducing these word confusions.

Rather than using a 'sounding out' strategy with beginning spellers, we would encourage an attitude of *inventing* spellings. Thus learners can use not just sounding out approaches, but also visual and structural ones as well.

'If you learn the rules, you'll be able to spell.'

There *are* regularities and conventions in English spellings and this information can be helpful for some students learning to spell. For example, the knowledge that the 'ly' suffix is always tacked on to the end of a whole word, e.g. love-ly, can be very useful. (See Resource Sheet 3.)

Unfortunately, most 'rules' in English are not rules at all but *regularities*. For every rule, there seems to be an exception. Or, the rule is so involved that students cannot remember the entire rule. For example, most of us remember "'i" before "e" except after "c"'. The additional part we forget is 'except when sounded like "a" as in neighbour and weigh'.

Most spellers who are 'catchers' never memorise rules. They learn the conventions and then memorise the words that are exceptions. However, we have found that showing students these regularities in words can be helpful. One way of doing this is by encouraging students to learn patterns of words. For example, we might link words of similar construction ('found', 'sound', 'round', etc.) on a student's spelling list. This helps to develop a sense of structure and relieves memorising stress.

'Look it up in the dictionary.'

Dictionary skills are useful in some contexts, but of limited applicability with beginning spellers or students with spelling difficulties. Many students have had only frustrating experiences with dictionaries. If the student's guess at a spelling puts him or her in the wrong section (for example, 'inuff' for 'enough'), then a week spent in the 'I' section of the dictionary will only leave the student furious at words, writing and language in general.

Dictionaries are useful, however, for students who are making minor spelling errors such as 'independant' for 'independent'; 'compleatly' for 'completely'; 'seperate' for 'separate', etc.

We recommend that less emphasis be placed on correctness in spelling than on better guesses. Students who have significant spelling problems or who are beginning writers should be encouraged to invent spellings and then given a correct version if the piece needs to be rewritten.

'Disguise your spellings with messy handwriting.'

Many students have cleverly figured out that their spelling difficulties can be disguised through sloppy handwriting. Criticism about conscious errors, such as messy handwriting, is somehow more tolerable than criticism about bad spelling. There may be some truth in this. Learners may indeed be able to 'slip some errors by the teacher'. Unfortunately, this approach does not help students learn how to spell. It continues to confuse the learners and leave them with a fuzzy visual image of many words. Not only that, but the students also acquire poor handwriting skills in addition to poor spelling skills.

Good handwriting can help a student learn spellings. Students should not abuse this skill but develop it to their advantage so that spelling can be improved, not made worse.

'I don't want to learn to write, I just want to learn to spell.'

Spelling cannot be learned in isolation. Unless we are regularly writing the words we want to learn to spell, we cannot be expected to remember them. We need practice, context, understanding and motivation in order to learn.

Unless students commit themselves to a programme of writing with spelling, they will find spelling boring, repetitive and unrewarding. Words will be difficult to memorise and very easy to forget. Writing provides us with the words for the spelling list. Without the writing, we have no need for the spellings.

'Why bother? Good spelling isn't important. It's the ideas that count.'

Ideas and the context of what we write are clearly far more important than the technical excellence of a piece of writing. However, good spelling actually helps writers in several ways. First, writers gain confidence in their own writing because they *know* the execution is correct. Confidence in writing helps fluency to develop.

Second, when we no longer have to stop and think about how a word is spelled, but can execute the spelling unconsciously, then our fluency increases and the emphasis on *composing* can take place. If we have to stop constantly and try to recall how a word is constructed, we lose the thread of our thought and the writing and thinking processes become frustrating.

Third, we know from how readers predict a text that when we are slowed down in the reading process (having to decode unconventional spellings, for example), we become frustrated with what we are reading. Not surprisingly, we become critical of the writer if the reading is too irritating or frustrating. Good spelling helps the reader; poor spelling hinders the reader.

Activity 2.6   Why is Spelling Important?

Purpose: To explore students' attitudes and feelings about spelling when approaching the subject from a reader's point of view and to illustrate why spelling matters and how poor spelling affects the reader.

1 Give students copies of one of the pieces of student writing on Resource Sheet 4 or an example of your own.

2 Ask them to read and consider the piece of writing and then, as a group, discuss:
  ● how they responded to it as a piece of writing (for example, what was good about it, what was not so good about it, how would they 'mark' it?)
  ● how the spelling errors affected them (for example, did they make it harder to read or understand? did it make them think less of the quality of the writing?)

Research has suggested that people tend to judge the content of a piece of writing partly by spelling accuracy. When two groups of London college students were given the same piece of writing – one with a number of misspellings and the other spelled accurately – the group with the misspelled version judged the content to be poorer than did the group with the accurately spelled version. This is a useful point to bring out in discussion as many students feel, not unjustly, that their writing is judged primarily on their spelling performance.

'You'll put students off if you correct their spelling.'

Red marks on a page are often the reason why many students give up in school. Students in adult education again and again relate experiences of teachers who underlined or corrected all the errors or mistakes in a piece of writing which made the student feel useless and worthless, not just as a writer, but as a person.

Nonetheless, all students understand that their writing will have mistakes. They find it patronising for teachers to say, 'Spelling doesn't matter' because they know that in the real world it does. If no corrections are made, students will either feel their work is unworthy of attention or that it is all correct. Either way, they are not helped in the learning process.

Teachers and students need to agree on a marking method which is helpful to both (see Chapter 14 on p. 38). Students may need help in identifying mistakes, proofreading, learning spellings and identifying what are 'good' errors and what are 'bad' errors. A particular focus on a particular type of error may be negotiated for each lesson or time period.

These are only a few of the misconceptions about spelling and the spelling system that students frequently mention. Sometimes, teachers can get students to add to the 'myths' list as they learn more about the English spelling system and how it works. Discussion about these myths should be ongoing. Teachers may need to refer back to the myths time and time again before students accept that their half-truths are not whole truths.

Attitudes to spelling

'Every year my report card said "needs work in spelling" but no one ever helped me learn!'

'It's not being able to spell the easy words that makes you feel so dumb.'

'They used to tell me to "watch my spelling". I did and nothing ever happened.'

'They decided I was thick 'cause I couldn't spell. So they put me in the back of the class and forgot about me.'

Usually, it's the student who realises the *status* of good spelling. One student told a story of losing her purse at work. She wanted to post a sign on the door to find out if anyone had seen it. She couldn't figure out how to spell 'purse' and ended up more distressed about that than losing her purse!

Spelling, in the real world, matters. If you can't fill out an application form, you don't get the job. If you can't write a letter of complaint, you can't be compensated. If you can't write an observation, you can't pass your child care course. If you can't write a supervisor's report, you don't get promoted. To minimise the importance of accuracy in communication is to belittle and ridicule the student's real experience in the world.

Some teachers and literacy tutors tell students that spelling doesn't matter. They decry the value put on spelling and ignore it. They only judge the content of what is written. Unfortunately, the evidence suggests that the rest of the 'real' world rarely feels this way and that people are commonly judged on the presentation of their work rather than on its content.

Teachers must be sensitive to these realities and not patronise students. Literacy development *must* include helping students learn to spell. It must also include acknowledging their past and current frustrations with the process.

How do students feel about their spelling?
It feels stupid

Again and again, learners have expressed how frustrating it feels not to be able to spell. People who are good spellers don't seem to understand that spelling isn't always as easy as it looks.

Unfortunately, many times teachers will have reinforced these feelings of inferiority. They, too, believe students must lack intelligence if they can't spell.

It feels shameful

Students with spelling problems often feel ashamed of their difficulties. They cover up their spelling problems by putting off writing, not handing in written assignments and by disguising poor spelling with poor handwriting.

In spite of all these strategems, students feel, somehow, that their spelling problems are *their* fault and *their* stigma. They rarely blame the school system, especially since they are unaware that they could have been taught any differently.

It feels frustrating

Since students have rarely been offered appropriate strategies for learning spellings, many of them have few examples or experiences of success in spelling and writing. Their only interaction with spelling has been negative and failure oriented.

Spelling success *must* be a part of the learning programme. Otherwise, students will give up on the process and either drop out or refuse to learn.

Nothing can work

Because of their negative past experiences, some students may feel they are 'unteachable', that nothing can work with them. If the teacher *believes* in the value of a spelling programme and if that spelling programme incorporates appropriate learning strategies and supports, the student will make progress and most of these negative attitudinal problems can be overcome with time, sometimes surprisingly quickly. However, teachers and tutors need to be sensitive to students' learning histories and past frustrations. A backlog of learning successes may be needed before students can begin to believe in their own potential.

Activity 2.7 **Talking about Spelling**

Purpose: To provide students and teachers with a record of how their thinking and feelings about spelling develop over time.

Refer to the sections on 'Attitudes' and 'Myths'. Give each student a small notebook to be used as a spelling journal.

At the beginning of the term, have each student enter in the journal their own feelings, attitudes, and myths about spelling. Every six weeks ask students to add to these entries. Use the journals for discussion about how spelling attitudes have changed and whether any benefits have accrued. (This is a method commonly used in schools with reading and writing journals.)

Activity 2.8   Spelling Histories

Purpose: To encourage students to think about their personal spelling histories and attitudes towards spelling.

Give students copies of Resource Sheet 5 and ask them to respond to these questions. Having a written record of their experiences and attitudes will help students to assess where they need to make improvements/employ new strategies. Alternatively, with literacy students who are non-writers, these questions could be used for group discussion rather than being written.

③
Learning Styles and Preferences

As learners, we all have preferred modes or styles of learning. Unfortunately, teachers and even other learners do not always share our own approach. Therefore, many learners are embarrassed or ashamed about the learning strategies they use. These students don't realise that *any learning strategy that works* is the right one. Too often, the best or most appropriate learning strategy has been abandoned in favour of one that the teacher appears to approve. Learners need to be supported in identifying which approaches are most fitted to their learning styles.

Many students find that if they understand their learning style preferences, they can better understand the kind of errors they make in spelling. (See pp. 11–12 for more information about error analysis.) Once students understand the kinds of errors they are likely to make and their own preferred style of learning, they can better choose appropriate learning strategies.

Most people would group learning preferences into these general categories:

Visual

Learners with a visual style will tend to 'see words in their heads'. They may feel they need to see them on paper to learn them. They prefer to read information in order to understand it.

Auditory

Learners with an auditory style will often need to talk about a topic or repeat information aloud in order to learn it. Sounding out words is often the favoured spelling approach for these learners.

Motor (or physical, sometimes referred to as kinaesthetic)

Learners with a motor or kinaesthetic style need to practise or do an activity in order to learn it. These students would need to write out words to learn them. The muscle movement of their bodies is their strongest learning mode. Some students have reported that tracing words with their forefinger has helped them learn to read.

Most of us are not rigid in our preferences and might use a number of approaches or strategies when trying to learn something new. However, many students do not realise that people do use a variety of ways to learn and that no particular approach is the 'right' one.

Identifying preferences

Students *unconsciously* identify their own learning preferences. Through observation, error analysis and practice, students will discover which approaches are most likely to succeed or match their own learning style. Some of the activities in this section are designed to help students see whether they are *visual, auditory* or *motor* learners. Just because we have a preferred learning style does not mean we cannot use a variety of learning methods. However, if students are encountering learning problems, knowing or being able to utilise their own learning style can help.

Applying other methods

Just because we have a *preferred* learning style does not mean we cannot use other learning styles. Most learners, in fact, can happily learn some words visually, others auditorally and others by the feel of writing them. Nonetheless, it is quite a relief for students to understand that just because others learn in a certain way, it does not mean that they must learn in that same way.

Other factors affecting learning

There are clearly many other factors, beyond the scope of this book, that influence learning and that shouldn't be overlooked; however, our emphasis here is more on cognitive style than on personal attitudes or history.

It is important for teachers to be aware that students function with a variety of learning styles which may be different from that of the teacher. Both learners and teachers may need to accommodate each others' styles. However, it can be helpful for both to understand that individual preferences may also include the following cognitive styles.

(These descriptions are taken from the work of A. F. Gregorc who has developed a measurement scale to help identify cognitive learning styles.)

Concrete Sequential Learner

This learner needs a structured approach to learning (this includes specific schedules and stated requirements) along with clear expectations of performance. Timetabling regular spelling reviews and making clear the number of words to be learned per week will be important for this student.

Abstract Sequential Learner

This learner works best on his or her own. He or she is able to formulate theories and is expert at research and learning from books. Structured learning is also helpful to this student. Some one-to-one work may be essential to help this learner acquire spelling strategies and concepts.

Abstract Group Learner

This learner works best in groups. Clarifying thinking through discussion with others is the way he or she learns best. He or she doesn't need the parameters of fixed schedules and may even prefer open-ended assignments. This learner will enjoy the interaction with other students and may even become a leader in getting other students involved in spelling discussions.

Concrete Group Learner

This learner needs concrete experiences to reinforce learning. Practising spellings and evidence from weekly spelling tests will be a high motivator for this learner. This learner may be able to generalise his or her learning to and from other experiences and should be encouraged to do so.

All learners may not fall neatly into any one of these categories. However, it is useful for students to understand that their own particular learning style may not match that of the teacher. Sometimes this can explain why some teachers appear more difficult to learn from than others. If teachers become more aware of the variety of learning preferences that students bring to the class, then they are more likely to be able to amend their own teaching approach to accommodate other kinds of learners.

If students become more aware of their own learning styles, they realise that other strategies may be necessary to learn the information teachers are presenting. For example, a teacher is a concrete sequential learner and so teaches in this style. A

learner is an abstract group learner. This student must learn to construct opportunities for discussion (even out of class time) if he or she is to learn this subject.

Activity 3.1   Identifying Your Learning Style

Purpose: To help students determine whether their *preferred* learning style is visual, auditory or motor kinaesthetic.

Have students complete the questionnaire on Resource Sheet 6. Students should realise that the answers will not always reflect their preferred learning style. For example, some sentences will be completed in every column. Nevertheless, a pattern of preference should emerge.

Discussion of the results should centre around the questions that follow the questionnaire.

Activity 3.2   How Do You Learn?

Purpose: To encourage students to analyse their own learning approaches and experiences and to explore the different ways we learn and remember different things (for example, observing, practising, memorising).

Discuss the following questions with your students. Questions 3–5 should emphasise the skills needed to learn something. They refer to general learning, not just academic material. Question 6 looks at other influences such as practice, motivation, time, etc. This questionnaire could also be used for students to interview each other in pairs.

1 Ask students to name three things they have learned to do in the last two years.

2 How did they learn to do them?

3 Ask students to name three things they're good at doing. When they learned these things, did they go about doing it in the same way?

4 Ask them to name one thing they find difficult to learn. What's hard about it? In what way is it different from the things they're good at learning?

5 What kind of skills do students think are needed in order to succeed at the things they find difficult to learn?

6 What qualities (besides skills) do they need in order to learn something? Can these be taught?

4

Analysing Errors

It is helpful for all learners to understand what kind of errors they are most likely to make. Once they have identified these, students are more likely to be able to adapt, and adopt learning strategies appropriate to their learning style.

You can easily carry out error analysis in the classroom. Be sure you have introduced spelling to the class through some of the activities in Chapters 1, 2 and 3.

First, teachers need to discuss their objectives in teaching error analysis and explain how it will help students learn to spell. These objectives may be itemised as follows:

1 Error analysis shows students what generalities and patterns there are to their mistakes.

2 It reinforces the point that English is not totally irregular and that students still have some myths about spelling. Students are often surprised that there is a 'logic' to their errors and this discovery increases their confidence.

3 It also helps them develop methods for correcting errors and learning the accurate spelling.

Second, teachers need to give students experience in analysis that doesn't involve correcting their *own* work. They need to learn the skill of analysis without the anxiety of correcting or judging their own work. So, teachers should use samples of other students' writing (from other classes or previous years) for their initial error analysis.

Finally, students can experiment with identifying and categorising their own errors to determine if their mistakes do follow a pattern and if particular difficulties seem to be a part of their spelling problem.

Types of errors made

As a rough guide, students should sort their errors into the five categories described below. Students may make errors of all types, but we have found it useful to identify the most common and frequent ones. Students whose errors fall mostly into category 1 are well on the way to understanding how to spell correctly. A high frequency of errors in categories 4 and 5 indicates that more severe difficulties are being encountered.

1   Spells it like it sounds

This means that most of the errors are close to spelling precedent and correspond to common English letter patterns. Example: 'serched' for 'searched', 'frend' for 'friend', 'terned' for 'turned'. A student whose errors are mainly of this type is well on the way to learning to spell.

2   Don't know rule

Errors of this type show that a student has not acquired an awareness of common rules or generalisations. Example: 'studys' for 'studies', 'shoping' for 'shopping', 'shage' for 'shaggy'.

3   Get letters out of order

Frequent errors of this kind indicate that a student has difficulty sequencing sounds or letter patterns. Example: 'frist' for 'first', 'flim' for 'film', 'vioce' for 'voice, 'interput' for 'interrupt'.

4   Mix up sounds

If errors of this type are common, the student may have difficulty discriminating sounds and/or remembering sound-symbol correlations. Example: 'sreet' for 'street', 'capalled' for 'collapsed', 'axcely' for 'actually', 'chunce' for 'chance', 'imediale' for 'immediately'.

5   Miss out or add bits

Errors of this type may show that the student has difficulty 'holding' sounds or keeping track of multisyllabic words. Example: 'rember' for 'remember', 'indual' for 'individual', 'beging' for 'beginning', 'folling' for 'following'. (There may also be errors of perseveration: adding syllables or repeating letter combinations as in 'beginining' for 'beginning'.)

We suggest doing a number of activities in categorising errors until students feel confident that they can analyse their own errors.

When one student discovered most of her errors went under 'mix up sounds', she was greatly relieved. 'Yes, it's true, I *can't* hear the sounds right!' She was then able, with great ease, to begin to develop visual strategies for learning spellings and her frustration decreased considerably.

(Teachers wishing to carry out a detailed analysis to assess student's specific difficulties should see p. 26.)

Activity 4.1 — Analysing Errors

Purpose: To help students learn to categorise their own errors and to develop links between the kind of error that is made and solutions to learning spellings for that word.

Part 1

1 Provide students with an analysis chart (see Resource Sheet 7b) and a sample of student writing containing a number of different kinds of errors or use Resource Sheet 7a.

2 Discuss the categories so that the students understand the kind of error that will go in each column.

3 Ask students to identify the errors in the piece of student writing and to categorise them on the analysis chart. This can be done in small groups or pairs.

4 Discuss the students' responses and why they entered certain words in certain categories.

Part 2

1 Have students categorise their own errors.

2 Discuss with students what kinds of spelling methods they might feel would work for errors in each column.

3 Have students choose several words from their categories and learn them in the manner discussed in point 2 above.

SECTION II: THE SPELLING PROGRAMME

Introducing the Programme

Why this method?

Most students have never been taught a way of learning to spell; more often they have been given lists of words to go away and learn. Although some students do 'catch' spelling in this way, many do not. For any spelling programme to be effective, then, especially when a student has not been able to 'catch' spelling, the following aspects must be addressed:

● **The programme must be meaningful.** It should be related to the students' *need* to spell and be based on words they use or want to use in their own writing.

● **The programme must be individualised.** It is essential that not only the particular words but also the strategies for learning the words are selected and adapted to fit the students' own spelling style.

● **The programme must be multi-sensory.** Students must be encouraged to use all their senses – visual, auditory and kinaesthetic/motor – to reinforce one another and to enable them to discover and emphasise their strongest mode of learning.

● **The programme must be structured.** Regularity and consistency help students to develop an awareness of word patterns over time and to build a spelling vocabulary that they can use in their writing.

● **The programme must be limited.** Students need time to absorb letter groupings and to make links between similar words. Therefore, not too many different letter patterns should be taught in any one lesson.

For the spelling programme to be effective, students must also be regularly producing free writing from which spellings can be selected to be learned on a weekly basis.

Steps to learning

Before they begin any spelling programme, students must understand the issues which they will need to tackle in order to improve their learning. Unless they are willing to explore and accept these underlying principles about how to learn, their spelling progress is likely to be impeded. Therefore, teachers should discuss at some length with students the following steps to learning:

1 Power to the student

The words chosen for the students' spelling lists must come from their own writing. If the words are taken from students' own writing, their motivation will be higher and they will have a sense of control over the learning process because they have been instrumental in deciding which words are to be learned. For the same reason, students should understand that they need to find their own best way of remembering words. This encourages students to become *active* learners.

2 Inventing spellings

As a first step in the spelling programme, students should develop a piece of writing without copying words or looking them up in the dictionary, 'inventing' a spelling where they are uncertain. (Spelling research indicates that guessing at spellings does not negatively affect the learner's ability to acquire a correct final version.) Since many students will have avoided words they can't spell or looked up every word in the dictionary before using it, they may have difficulty taking the risk of guessing at words. They need to understand that if we make a guess at how a word is spelled, even if it is wrong, we are attempting to apply to print what we know about the English language; that is, we are forming a hypothesis, or theory, about a spelling. This 'having a theory' about something makes us more likely to remember an amendment or correction to our guess than to remember a spelling we have never attempted. Thus guessing helps learning.

Activity 5.1   **Inventing Spellings**

Purpose: To give students experience of and confidence in inventing spellings by looking at how much they already know about English spelling.

1 Ask students to invent a spelling for the word 'orlop' (a real word, but one few of us have seen used).

2 List on the board all the alternatives suggested. (Some common ones are aulop, awlop, allop.)

3 Discuss why students chose to spell it the way they did. Points to bring out are:
   ● Students have unconscious knowledge about spellings – nearly everyone past beginner stage can make a reasonable guess.

- There isn't a 1:1 correlation between sound and symbol, but there are only a certain number of likely possibilities.
- Spelling is largely visual – you can only know for certain how to spell a word by seeing it.

4 Now have students write a story or description in class, using at least ten words they don't know how to spell and inventing spellings for them.

5 List some of the words they attempted and discuss them with reference to the points in step 3 above.

This activity was inspired by Olwen Smith.

Students are often amazed at how many words they can spell correctly, or nearly correctly when they allow themselves to invent spellings. Most students who have some familiarity with print can make sufficient guesses at the beginnings and endings of words, although their understanding or memory may be vague for the middle parts.

3 Analysing the error

Once a student attempts a spelling, the teacher and student can then compare the invented spelling with the correct version. They can analyse which part has already been unconsciously learned and which part will need to be memorised. If students recognise that only certain sections of a word need to be learned, this is less intimidating than the feeling that thousands of words must be learned before they can spell with confidence. Through this process, students also learn to discriminate between 'good' errors (those which follow English spelling convention) and 'bad' errors (those which do not), based on a growing understanding of likely alternatives in the English writing system. (For instance, they learn that the sound 'shun' at the end of a word is never spelled 'shun', and is most likely to be spelled 'tion'.)

4 Practising

Students must practise in the new, agreed way (see the Look, Cover, Write, Check Method, p. 20). Merely copying words or trying to memorise them in an old way will not help students to learn the words. First, students must realise that spelling is primarily a *visual/motor activity*. To spell a word correctly we first need a visual image of it. This is why we can copy a word over and over and still not be able to spell it – and why we do not become good spellers by reading a lot. In order to be able to spell a word, the students must actually look at it with *interest* and with the *intention* of remembering it.

We also remember the spelling of a word by the feel of our hand writing it. Students can try writing their names with their eyes closed to experience this for themselves (see the activity on the Motor Memory, p. 17).

In order to get a visual image of the word, we need *actively* to try to remember how it looks. This is why the student must cover it up during the practising process. Students need to understand that it is not helpful to 'peek' when they are unsure of part of the word as they will never get a complete image of the whole word this way.

Finally, checking the word back, letter by letter is as important, if not more so, than all the other steps in the method. If students find their mistake and correct it by writing the *whole word* correctly, they are much more likely to remember the correct spelling the next time they practise. Again, it is important to rewrite the whole word (and not just insert letters) in order to make use of the motor memory.

5 Review and testing

Students will need weekly testing of words to determine which words have been learned and which will need additional practice. Short dictations based on words from previous spelling lists should be part of this review. Students who lack confidence in their ability to remember spellings also need this regular review of words to reinforce their experience of success – that they really *have* learned the words.

6
Selecting Words to be Learned

If students are to be active participants in their learning, they need to be involved in deciding which words they will learn each week. On the other hand, they are likely to want to learn only the long, interesting ones (for example, 'dinosaur', 'tyrannosaurus') and not the little boring ones so often misspelled (for example, 'does', 'there'). Negotiation is the key here, and a list which includes both sorts of words is the best for learning as it sets up a nice balance between being interesting without having too many difficult letter patterns to learn at once.

We normally suggest selecting 10–12 words per week, although some students may be able to learn up to 15 if words are grouped together as suggested. We don't generally advise learning more than this as memory loss over time is likely to be greater, especially if a number of different but similar letter patterns are involved, such as 'ou' and 'ow' words, '-ence' and '-ance' words, etc.

We recommend selecting words on the basis of the following criteria:

• They should be words that the student is highly motivated to learn.

• They should be words used frequently by the students.

• They should be words which the student needs only a little practice to perfect, i.e. their errors are close to the correct spelling.

• They should include common words: 'which', 'does', 'because', etc.; and words with common letter patterns: '-ight', '-ough', '-tion'. *It is important to build students' awareness of these.*

In selecting words, it is important to group them in ways which will encourage students to make links and generalisations.

Consequently, we suggest grouping words to be learned in the following ways:

a according to a common rule:

baby	babies
copy	copies

b according to letter patterns:

feet	come	ear
sweet	home	earn
meet	some	learn

It is sometimes useful to link words which look alike

but don't sound alike to emphasise the visual nature of spelling.

c according to prefixes and suffixes:

gener	ally	tele	vision
fin	ally	tele	phone
natur	ally	tele	scope

d with other members of a 'word family'. For instance if the student wants to learn 'independence' it is useful to build it up

in	de	pend	ence	dis	satis	faction
	de	pend			satis	fy
	de	pend	ence		satis	faction

This system helps students break away from a tendency to rely too much on spelling by sounding out.

Finally, a word of warning:

Never present words in the same week with easily confused letter sequences or sound patterns, for example,

> here and hear
> '-sion' and '-tion' words
> '-ise' and '-ice' words
> form and from

It is advisable only to group words in twos or threes at most. Otherwise, the student is faced with memorising a long list of similar words which looks boring and tends to dissipate interest.

Activity 6.1 **Selecting Words for the Spelling List**

Purpose: To encourage students to think strategically about selecting and grouping words in order to learn them effectively.

Use Resource Sheet 8 on *Selecting Words to Learn*.

I Talk through the examples on the Resource Sheet with the class. Be sure students know what a 'root' word is.

2 Suggest students find similar examples in their own writing. These examples can be put on the board. Discuss as a class ways of grouping the words or linking them with other words.

3 Suggest students each make up a list of ten words to learn from their own writing. This can be done in pairs, with students helping each other to link and group words.

4 Look at the lists and discuss any misunderstandings, confusions or issues that arise.

7
Strategies for Remembering Spellings

If students are to become successful learners, they will need to find strategies for remembering spellings which work for *them*. Finding out about their own learning styles (as discussed in Chapter 4) is a useful introduction to talking about ways of remembering spellings. Understanding and exploring how memory works will also prepare students for looking at words in a 'strategic' way. Discussing different ways of breaking up a word in a group is also a good way to help students discover effective strategies.

Memory and learning

At this point it might be useful to discuss how an understanding of the way our memory works can help us become better learners.

It is useful to explain the difference between short-term or 'working' memory and long-term memory (see Resource Sheet 9). We store information we want to remember in our long-term memory. Highly meaningful information, like important experiences or events in our own lives, is easily retrieved from the long-term memory. Other information may be less easy to retrieve. However, in order to spell fluently, we need to store and retrieve words from our long-term memories.

Our short-term memory is used to recall information immediately after we have attended to it. For example, we use short-term memory to recall a telephone number long enough to dial, or to remember a passage we have just read. Some students may have difficulty holding more than two or three letters in their short-term memory long enough to write them down. Even then, these students may not remember the letters or their order unless they are consciously memorising them.

If the memorisation is *meaningful*, i.e. we can associate it with something we already know, then we can store the information in our long-term memory. Then, if it is organised effectively, we can retrieve it when we want to.

In order to write fluently, we need already to know how words are spelled so that we do not have to think about them. If we only copy words, we are using our short-term memory for a few letters at a time, just long enough to write down the word. However, with conscious practice which is relevant and organised, we can permanently remember and retrieve words, even if our short-term memories are limited.

Getting words into long-term memory takes time, and we have limits as to how much we can memorise at a time. Therefore, students should understand why they should not be expected to learn more than 10–15 words per week and should not try to learn more than this amount.

Another useful way of discussing memory is to look at the different methods we use to remember different sorts of things. For instance, we may have a visual image of a place we need to return to, or we may just remember the number and name of the street by reciting it to ourselves. Remembering how to ride a bicycle or to swim is very different from remembering a phone number. We remember physical things with our motor or muscle memory, which is very powerful. Although it takes a lot of practice to learn to swim, once we have learned we do not forget. Even if we don't swim for several years we will still remember how to do it when we are thrown in the water one day!

The problem with the motor memory is that it is also very difficult to *unlearn* something learned this way. For instance, if we learn a dance step wrongly, it is harder to unlearn it and relearn it correctly than it was to learn it in the first place. Since spelling is partly a motor activity, the hand remembers as well as the eye. If a student has been miswriting a word, the hand may continue to write that word incorrectly because it *feels* right.

Thus learners must not only get a correct visual image for a word, but may also need to retrain their hands to write it. Students need to understand how prior learning (or inaccurate learning) can affect the current learning situation. Students need not be embarrassed about misspelling 'simple' words or having difficulty learning commonly used words. They are frequently having to unlearn an old spelling at the same time as they are learning a new one. An awesome task!

Activity 7.1   Memory and Learning

Purpose: To look at the different ways we remember different sorts of things, distinguishing auditory, visual and motor memories.

Discussion should centre around the following or similar questions. The questions could be discussed as a group, or in pairs first.

I How would students find a friend's house they had been to only once or twice? Would they be able to *recall* how to get there? How? Would they *recognise* it when they arrived? How?

2 How do students remember a phone number? The name of an author? The title of a book?

3 How did students learn the alphabet? The months of the year?

4 How would students remember a film or television programme that they wanted to tell a friend about?

5 How do they remember how to get to school?

6 How did students learn to swim? Or ride a bike? Or do a special dance step?

7 a If they didn't ride a bike for a year or more, do students think they would still remember how to do it? How?

b If they didn't visit a friend's house for a year, do they think they would remember how to get there? How?

c If students didn't use a telephone number for a year or so, do they think they would remember it?

What is the difference between these three types of memory?

Activity 7.2   Memory and Spelling 1

Purpose: To make students aware of how we need to practise and review work to absorb information into the long-term memory.

Use the chart on Resource Sheet 10 as the basis for discussion. The following questions may bring out important issues and misconceptions.

1 When is the best time to practise something the first time?

2 How quickly do we forget most of what we learn if we don't practise or review it? Does this surprise students?

3 Would memorising a list of spellings over and over again one evening and then not looking at them again be a good way to remember them? Would just looking at them once be a good way? What *would* be a good way?

Activity 7.3   Memory and Spelling 2

Purpose: To help students using the Look, Cover, Write, Check Method (see p. 20) and to introduce to them the need to actively develop strategies for remembering spellings.

1 Use the examples below as the basis for a discussion of the eight points given on Resource Sheet 10:

a
sight	fin	ally
right	gradu	ally
bright	usu	ally
brighten		

b 'fat her' for 'father'

c words we want to learn because we use them in our writing

d so it is difficult to learn long lists of words

e for example, words we don't know the meaning of

f If we know that 'breakfast' means to break the fast, it is easier to remember.

g If we know from the word 'television' that 'tele' means far and 'vision' means seeing, then it is easier to learn 'telescope', 'telephone' and 'telecommunications'.

h for example, 'necessary' has one **c**ollar and two **s**ocks, or

'Towe**L**' as in the shape of a towel rack, or **B**ig **E**lephants **A**ren't **U**gly, they are BEAUTIFUL

2 Ask students to select some words (two or three) from their writing that they would like to learn and to experiment with ways of remembering them.

3 Suggest they work in pairs or groups of three and try to find as many ways as possible to remember the words.

Activity 7.4   Strategies for Memorising

Purpose: To explore the relationship between memory and learning so that students may understand how and why some strategies for remembering work better than others.

1 Using Resource Sheet 9, discuss the difference between long-term and short-term memory.

2 Put a list of 25–30 words on the board. (This should be suddenly 'revealed'.) Read through them with students, covering the words as you read them until they are all covered. Ask students which ones they remember and write these on the board. Uncover the original list and compare. Include on the list:

a concrete nouns, for example, table, sofa, magazine, saucepan, telephone, tulips, cabbage, aeroplane, garden

b abstract nouns, for example, idea, honesty, violence, friendship, democracy, science, capitalism, fear

c one or two unusual or funny words, for example, hippopotamus, apoplexy

d one or two emotionally powerful words, for example, sex, piss

e one or two famous persons, for example, Margaret Thatcher, Madonna, Picasso

f the name of your school, football team, town

3 Discussion should focus on the points to remember:

a *How* did students remember the words – did they make links or associations?

b *Why* were some words more easily remembered, for example, last words on the list (recency), significant words (value), unusual words?

Activity 7.5   The Motor Memory

Purpose: To help students realise the part the motor memory plays in remembering spellings.

1 Ask students to close their eyes and write their names.

2 Ask them to explain how they were able to do this. Discussion should centre around the following points:

- the 'feeling' of writing their name;
- how they could 'feel' it was *correctly* written;
- the need to write a word to learn it rather than just looking at it;
- how writing the whole word, and not just the bit you got wrong, can help you remember it;
- why joined-up handwriting is more helpful than printing in learning to spell.

Making words accessible

As spelling is primarily a visual skill, in the end we have to rely on knowing whether the word *looks* right. However, not everyone has a knack for visualising spellings. Consequently, we would recommend a number of ways to reinforce the visual image and make words more visually accessible.

Breaking up the word visually by using space and colour can help students 'chunk' bits of a word and also help focus on the bit they are misspelling.

For instance, a student wants to learn the word 'yesterday'. She already knows 'yes' and 'day', so writing it

yes/ ter/ day or

yes ter day

or highlighting the 'ter', makes it suddenly easy for her to see.

Some other examples are given on Resource Sheet 11.

In addition to reinforcing visualisation, we encourage students to experiment with different ways of breaking up words. For instance, one student who found it difficult to remember the word 'individual' found it helpful to understand its meaning – one which cannot be divided. So she learned it as:

divid/e
in divid ual

Another student, however, who tended, as she put it, to 'lose the middles' of words, found it easier to learn it as

ind ivi dual

because the 'middle' became a symmetrical visual pattern which locates the two 'i's for her.

For students who have difficulty keeping track of syllables or parts of words, tapping out the syllables with their fingers while saying and writing the word can help them coordinate the motor activity with the intended parts.

Students with poor visual memories generally benefit from:

1 the exaggerated *pronunciation* of words, for example, 'be/ca/use' for 'because'. Students are advised to make up a 'spelling pronunciation' for the word which will remind them of what the word *looks* like. This is very different from 'spelling it as it sounds'; rather it is 'sounding it as it is spelled'.

2 understanding the *structure* of words, for example, morphemes, root words, suffixes, prefixes, etc. as in

'sign', 'signal', 'signature'. This helps students move away from over-reliance on sound.

3 practising building on root words, for example,

point
appoint
dis appoint
dis appoint ment

We find that *students who have difficulties discriminating or 'holding' sounds* benefit from:

1 finding words within words, for example,

cap a city

fat her

Some students become very adept at this.

2 reinforcing visual memory through grouping and linking words of similar letter patterns, for example,

ease   sound
please   found
pleasure   round

6 breaking up words in a visually accessible way to compensate for weaknesses in keeping track of sounds, for example,

acc ommo dation

in v isi ble

All students benefit from using joined-up handwriting, even if they only join letters in twos and threes. This method reinforces the motor memory. Students should be encouraged to try joining up letters when they practise their spellings. They are often surprised when, as one student said, 'the word just flows'.

Activity 7.6   **Ways to Help Remember Spellings**

Purpose: To help students identify their preferred spelling strategies and also to try others which may work for them.

1 Give students Resource Sheet 11 on *Ways to Help Remember Spellings* and talk through each strategy.

2 Have students select five words from their own writing which they would like to learn.

3 Suggest they try at least three different ways (using the sheet) to remember each word.

4 Ask them to decide which strategy is easiest for each word. See if they can relate the strategies they picked to their preferred learning style.

This activity can also be done in pairs.

Activity 7.7 Students Talking About Spelling

Purpose: To explore different strategies for learning spellings.

1 Have students read Resource Sheet 12.

2 Discuss the different ways the students remember the words. Ask your students which ways they would find easiest. Note from the spelling of 'Gatqwick' in the transcript how much spelling relies on visualising.

3 As a group, select about five words relevant to your class and let students find different ways of breaking up the words. Suggest they work in pairs.

4 Gather the results and write them on the board. Alternatively, divide the class into groups or teams, the aim being to see which group can find the most ways to learn the words.

Activity 7.8   Word Building

Purpose: To give students practice in word building and to encourage them to see how words are structured as a way of using meaning or known words to help learn new words.

1 Talk through Resource Sheet 13 with your class. Note the meanings of the prefixes where appropriate. Clarify terms such as **root word**, **prefix**, **suffix** if these are not familiar.

2 Select some common root words and get students to practise word building as a group, writing the words on the board as they think of them.
Some examples are:

	divide			**scribe**			**sign**	
un	divid	ed	de	scribe		de	sign	
in	divid	ual		scribble		de	sign	ate
	divid	ends		script	ure		sign	ature
			pre	script	ion	as	sign	ment

Discuss the meanings of the words as you go along; for instance, an individual is one which cannot be divided.

3 In small groups or pairs, have students find examples of words in their own writing which they can break down in this way and find the root word. Have them see how many new words they can make from these roots.

A word about rules

Many teachers and students believe that learning rules is a good way to help with spelling, but we have not found this to be true. When children learn rules, they tend to overgeneralise, as in 'lookeded' and 'seed'; learning to apply rules appropriately is a part of learning the language. In spelling, this is much the same; rules are integrated through acquiring common spelling patterns, an understanding of word structures and a sense of where it is appropriate to use certain letters. How many of us know the rules for doubling letters? Yet we know how to spell such words as 'parallel', 'embarrass', 'accommodation', and we do this by seeing if the word looks right, not by following a rule. If we had to follow rules to remember spellings, we would slow down our writing considerably. It is much easier to write 'necessary' by remembering 'one *c*ollar and two *s*ocks' than by trying to remember some rule that might apply. Even with the popularity of the 'i before e except after c' rule, 'receive' and 'believe' are commonly misspelled; besides, it doesn't help us if we spell them 'receve' or 'belive'!

However, *finding* common 'rules' can help students become aware of regularities in English spelling and thus make guesses which are closer to spelling convention (see below).

Activity 7.9   Finding the Rule

Purpose: To give students the opportunity to find for themselves the regularities and exceptions in English spelling as an aid to learning.

Although learning rules is not usually a very successful strategy for *learning* spellings, finding regularities in English spelling helps students to devise their own hypotheses about spelling, and this has been shown to aid learning (see p. 4). It also encourages attention to the *details* of letter combinations. In addition, students remember best what they learn from *experience*.

1 Use Resource Sheet 3 on *Finding the Rule*. Look at the first example with your students and discuss the purpose of the exercise. Make sure they understand the terms **suffix** and **prefix**.

2 Divide the class into groups and give the groups 10–15 minutes for each set of examples, to find a rule. (They may need more or less time for different sets.)

3 Write the rules on the board and discuss.

4 To check students' ability to generalise from what they have done, ask them to spell other words which fit the rule, for example, 'likely' for the '-ly' rule.

If students cannot do this, it may be necessary to look at the examples again and make observations about what generalisations can be made. For some students, practising their 'own' words over a period of time is the only way they will begin to acquire such generalisations.

Note: Depending on the level of your class, you may only want to use parts of the Resource Sheet. You may also want to make up other sets of words for students to 'find the rule'.

8

Practising Spellings: The Look, Cover, Write, Check Method

The Look, Cover, Write, Check Method is based on the work of Margaret Peters. It is an extremely effective way of learning spellings because it stresses the visual motor nature of spelling and is multi-sensory, structured and adapted to an individualised approach.

This method, *if followed correctly*, works for almost all students. Students must, however, undertake to practise regularly at the prescribed intervals; otherwise, they will not learn their spellings.

Activity 8.1   **The Look, Cover, Write, Check Method**

Purpose: To introduce the Look, Cover, Write, Check Method to students, to clarify the steps in the method and clear up any misconceptions which emerge.

1 Use Resource Sheet 14 on The Look, Cover, Write, Check Method to talk through each step with the class. Points to emphasise:

a Having a small exercise book in which to practise spellings is highly recommended for keeping words in one place and having a 'word bank' to which students can refer. Otherwise, pages tend to get lost or misordered.

b It is extremely important that the words in the first column are checked by the teacher; many a student has ignored this rule, miscopied the word and consequently learned the miscopied version!

c Self-correcting is one of the most effective tools for learning, so it is necessary when practising the words to check *each* word back *letter for letter* and write the word correctly before going on to the next word.

d When correcting an error, students should be sure to write out the *whole* word correctly. Note the example on the handout.

e Above all, make sure students are clear about the difference between 'practising' and 'testing'!

2 Have students select two or three words from their own writing and practise them in class. Discuss how difficult they found it. Comments often come up like, 'This is too easy', 'How do I know I'll remember it?'

3 Have students make a list of 6–8 words from their own writing (see Chapter 6) and practise them in the prescribed way over the week.

4 The following week, test students in groups, or have them test each other in pairs. Discuss how successful they found the method and also any problems that came up.

Note: Some students will not be entirely successful until they have learned some strategies for remembering words, so this needs to be brought out in the discussion.

When you have introduced the method to your students, it is important to demonstrate:

• your confidence in the method and your belief that it will work for them in spite of their past failures;

• your interest and enthusiasm about words. Many teachers think of spelling as a 'boring' activity and may unwittingly communicate this attitude to their students. Talking about, looking at and noticing words generates enthusiasm and confidence in students. (See Resource Sheet 12 on *Students Talking About Spelling*.)

It is also essential to talk through each step of the method with the class and to explain why it is necessary to follow *all* the steps.

Below is an illustration of the Look, Cover, Write, Check Method. Note that this student decided he could remember the *eat* in 'create' better than his original attempt to divide the word. Note also that although he did have trouble with 'psyche' and 'psychology', in the end he got them right. (The ticks in the margin indicate words correctly spelled when tested; a cross indicates that the word was spelled wrong and a 'C' means the student corrected it himself.)

	a.s.a.p.	1 day later	2-3 days later
Source / Re source	Source	Source	Source
Tur moil	Resource	Resource	Ressurce
Matur·ity	turmoil	turmoil	turmoil
Pur chase	Maturity	maturity	maturity
create Cr eat / creative Creative	Purchase	purchase	purchase
psy ché	Creative / Create	create / Creative	Create / Creative
psy ché log y	psychy × Psyche	pysche × psyche	Psyche
dense	psychology	psychology	Psychology
tense	dense	dense / tension	dense
tension.	tense	tender	tense / tension.
tender / tender ness	tension / tender / tenderness	Tenderness	tender. / tenderness.

9

Testing and Reviewing

Although some students learn and retain spellings easily, many do not. It is therefore necessary each week to test the words which have been practised, and to follow this with a dictation a week later. This gives students the opportunity to review and consolidate spellings.

Have students learned the words on the spelling list?

Each week the words should be tested in the following way:

1 Each word is dictated to the student.

2 The student repeats the word aloud and then writes it.

3 The student spells the word back orally as it is written.

4 If a word has an error, ask the student to find it. Say, for example, 'Something's missing from that word. Can you find it?' If the error is not easily identified, do not let the student flounder. Display the correct spelling, compare it with the student's and discuss differences.

5 The student looks at the word again and writes it correctly from memory. This word is added to the next week's spelling list.

During the initial weeks of tuition, you may need to:

   a emphasise that the process takes time;
   b point out the progress made in recognising and correcting errors;
   c offer reminders about the method.

It is also useful to check students' spelling books to ensure they are following the method and to make any necessary suggestions.

Dictations

The purpose of the dictation is both to give students practice in writing the words they learned the *previous* week in context, and to check that they have retained the spellings. Sentences should be constructed from words students have demonstrated they know. More than one spelling word may be incorporated into each sentence and about five sentences each week should be given. Students can make up their own sentences in advance. Use this method:

1 Dictate the sentence.

2 The student repeats the sentence and then writes it from memory. If the sentence is too long, it may need to be dictated in chunks.

3 The student should proofread the sentence immediately and, if possible, correct any errors.

4 Point out any errors which have not been noticed. Encourage the student to correct them.

5 If an error is not corrected, show the correct version and ask the student to write it from memory.

6 Continue this process with each sentence.

Dictations help to identify:

- words the student finds hard to learn;
- easily confused sounds or sequences;
- strategies used to remember words.

They also help students to gain confidence in being able to retain and use words they have learned.

   If a student forgets a spelling and cannot easily correct it, that spelling should be added to the current list for review and practice. It is also helpful in this case to try a new way to remember the word.

Samples of Dictations

① She wash the bruisyed fruit and ruined
washed.
it.

② Soon it will be winetr and school will
be Cooled. Closed.   winter

③ The lady goes into the kitchen to Cook
a Steak for breakfast.   kitchen

④ The moon looked little on that winerty
night.   wintery

⑤ We whent they to cure the polo peoled
peoled. people.   went there

⑥ She put the Suarg and fruit juice in
a bowl and mixed it with a Spoon.
Sugar.
Mixed

This student has some difficulty retaining spellings. She seems to take a visual approach to spelling and have difficulty keeping track of the sounds. She appears to be aware of her problems and will try to attempt several spellings, as in 'sugar' and 'people'. Dictations allow her to attempt words she has practised and encourage her to increase her ability to predict where her errors lie.

I thought she appeared ~~anxious~~ but I listened
anxious
in the usual manner.

I often listen to excessively ~~towd~~ music.
loud

The wonderful rhythms of the band made
practise unne~~cessary~~.

The students were successful when they
~~occupyod~~ the Government offices.
occupied

The earnest young woman suggested we
remember our unusual Stories.

The student above has been unable to generalise from 'usual', which she spelled correctly, to 'unusual', where she omitted a 'u'. She needs to be encouraged to develop better proofreading skills. Dictations are an opportunity for her to do this.

On the next page is a sample of the three steps in Ann's spelling programme.

Figure (i) is Ann's spelling book, showing the way she has broken up the words to learn and her attempts to learn the words over the week. As you can see, she is already having problems with 'distasteful' and fails to check it adequately. When she is tested on the words (ii), she has to make two attempts at 'already' and goes back to an old spelling of 'like'. However, though she struggles with 'distasteful', it is with the ending rather than the 'e' in the middle. A week later, sentences containing her words are dictated to her (iii). Once again, she has trouble with 'already', this time with remembering it is one word. When she attempts 'ready', however, she not only inserts an 'e' again, but her persistent 'b/d' confusion re-emerges and seems to take over. In 'distasteful', again she omits and then confuses the position of the middle 'e'.

Ann has difficulty retaining a visual image of a word and recognising the correct spelling. She also seems unable to stop her hand taking over and writing an 'old', incorrect, sequence of letters or letter reversal. She needs to be more conscientious about checking spellings when she practises them. She also needs some help with paying more attention to word families, i.e. always making sure that she has written the *whole* of 'taste' before adding the 'ful'. Ann might also benefit from linking other 'al-' words, for example, 'also', 'almost', 'always'. Her joined-up script should help her with her 'b/d' confusions in time, but changing motor habits is a slow process. Reminding herself with a mnemonic, for example, '**d** starts in the mi**d**dle', may also help.

	a.s.p.	1 day	2-3 days
✓ ready	ready ✓	ready ✓	ready ✓
already	alreadeys already ✓	already ✓	already ✓
more	more ✓	more ✓	more ✓
before	before ✓	before ✓	before ✓
whether (or not)	whether ✓	whether ✓	whether ✓
would	would ✓	would ✓	would ✓
could	could ✓	could ✓	could ✓
should	should ✓	should ✓	
like	like ✓	like ✓	like ✓
dislike	dislike ✓	dislike ✓	dislike ✓
taste	taste ✓	taste ✓	taste ✓
distaste	distaste ✓	distaste ✓	distaste ✓
✗ distasteful	✗ distastful ✓	✗ dislasful	distastful ✓
✓ done.	done done ✓	done ✓	d done ✓

Figure (i)

⌐ ready
+ alredy
✓ already
⌐ more

⌐ before
⌐ whether
⌐ would
⌐ could
⌐ should
✗ lisfie   like
⌐ dis like
⌐ taste
✓ distaste
✗ distastefule
distz
distastefutz
⌐ distastefol.
⌐ done

Figure (ii)

12th
March

I have ~~all ready gone~~ that more times
them you   already   done

I dislike the taste of this ~~the~~ this ~~clinor~~
                                          clinner

She wondered whether the ~~children~~ would be
                                     children
~~reatey~~ in time
reades
reachy

Could you find a more ~~distastful~~ pictur
                                   distasefol
~~before~~ tomorrow
~~before~~ before

distasful   distasteful
                 distasteful

before

They should know ~~about~~ ~~this~~ ~~our~~ ower
                      about   our
distaste for this

Figure (iii)

10
Specific Strategies for Specific Difficulties

In this section we offer a number of strategies which our experience has shown work with students who have specific learning difficulties (commonly referred to as 'dyslexia'). Once students are aware of the learning approaches they need, they should be encouraged to employ those approaches *all the time.* Students with specific difficulties are likely to have a 'shotgun' approach to learning. They use one approach for a little while and abandon it, then they try out another. When a diagnosis or error analysis reveals particular weaknesses, students should be encouraged to adopt methods which utilise their *strengths.*

It should be noted that all students with specific difficulties do not all have the same particular problems. However, most students have a combination of difficulties, and learning through print is an especially onerous task for these individuals. These are the main areas of difficulty most encountered:

Memorising difficulties

Many students with specific learning difficulties have trouble with rote memorising tasks. This does not mean they cannot memorise, but rather that they need more time, more energy and greater concentration to memorise lists, numbers, information and spelling words. Students need to understand that it is the combination of memorising and perceptual problems that are inhibiting success.

Because of these innate memorising problems, these learners *must understand* the nature of their spelling difficulties, how they affect their learning of particular words, and why certain learning strategies will help them more than others. Once students have this understanding, they are less likely to be as frustrated and are usually willing to invest the extra time needed to make progress in spelling.

Perceptual processing confusions

The most common processing difficulties which impair spelling performance are those in visual processing, auditory processing and motor integration. It is important to bear in mind that if a student has perceptual processing difficulties, this does not mean that there is something wrong with his or her seeing or hearing. The eye or the ear may be working adequately and the student can still have *processing* problems in specific sensory areas.

Whether the perceptual confusion is constitutional or habitual in nature is for most students irrelevant. Most students, however, find it helpful to be told how their particular difficulty will affect their learning and what can be done about it. Teachers will find the better they understand error analysis and learning styles, the clearer and more specific they can be in discussions with students.

General language and learning problems

Many dyslexic students experience continued language difficulties in composing (due to word finding problems), sequencing (determining 'correct' order), grammar (especially word confusions) and proofreading (identifying and correcting their own errors). Mechanical skills such as copying and consistency in handwriting style can also cause problems. These problems can persist for dyslexic students *in spite of adequate tuition.*

Dyslexic students commonly confess that they have trouble making generalisations about language learning and these aspects of learning have an impact on learning spellings. Patterns of words are not automatically integrated or consciously acquired. Dyslexic students do not easily 'see' similarities in structure between words. They may need considerable help in learning to 'chunk' words and develop methods for grouping sounds and/or letters.

Most learners have had negative experiences in learning to spell in school. They are often resistant to practising their spelling words. Nonetheless, learners with specific difficulties must realise that *only* by regular and consistent practice will new spellings be acquired. Some students find that practising their spellings at least five times a week, rather than the three times necessary for most learners, is a better way to get into the consistent routine needed to learn new words.

Analysing spelling styles and errors

As discussed in Chapter 4 (see p. 11), error analysis can be useful for any student undertaking a spelling programme. When working with a student with specific difficulties, however, it is our experience that an analysis of learning style and problems is *imperative.*

It is important for both teacher and student to understand the kind of errors students with specific difficulties are likely to make. The error can then be compared to the correct version and students can see the nature of their learning styles and identify their strengths and weaknesses.

Ideally, students with specific difficulties should have a full diagnosis which includes analysis of their reading, writing and spelling problems. However, an analysis of spelling errors can only be helpful to the student with specific difficulties and also to the teacher.

How to carry out an error analysis

Errors can be collected from a piece of free writing or a draft of an essay, story, etc. In many instances, students with specific difficulties, especially adults or older adolescents, rely so heavily on dictionaries or on only writing words they can spell correctly, that teachers may have problems identifying a sufficient number of mistakes to complete an error analysis. Therefore, we have often used a short dictation to elicit a number of errors. A dictation also enables the teacher or tutor to see how a student might guess or 'invent' a spelling. At least 20–25 errors need to be analysed to observe a pattern of errors.

Diagnostic dictation

The following dictation is taken from *Diagnostic and Remedial Spelling* by Margaret Peters and can be given to a group. (See the same book for dictations at other levels.) The teacher should be careful to dictate slowly and clearly and repeat frequently if asked. Students are free to self-correct, but should be encouraged to guess at words even if they feel the spellings are incorrect.

> Late one night my friend woke me saying, 'Would you enjoy a trial run in my new helicopter?' I had scarcely scrambled into my track suit before we were away. The lights of the city glowed beneath, the stars above. I was beginning to wonder about our destination, when I caught sight of the spinning knife edge of the surface of what must have been a type of flying saucer whistling round us. We dodged skilfully to avoid an accident. To our relief, the space craft regained height and we sank down to earth and the comfortable bed I had never actually left.

Categorising the error

We have used five categories of error:

1 Logical phonetic alternatives which follow English spelling convention: 'hart' for 'heart', 'seet' for 'seat', 'mension' for 'mention'.

2 Visual sequencing errors: 'dose' for 'does'; 'Britian' for 'Britain'.

3 Rule oriented errors which do not follow English spelling convention: 'citys' for 'cities', 'jock' for 'joke', 'stashun' for 'station'.

4 Auditory perceptual errors; sounds missing or confused: 'scelye' for 'scarcely', 'srambling' for 'scrambling'; 'natul' for 'natural'.

5 Motor integration; repeating or adding or telescoping parts of words: 'beginining' for 'beginning', 'rember' for 'remember'. Also, omitting or adding letters *unintentionally*.

See p. 31 for an example of an Error Analysis Sheet.

Many students will have errors in several categories. (It would be unusual, however, for a student to have errors in *all* categories.) What the teacher and student are looking for is *patterns* of errors which seem to indicate consistent weaknesses. In general, we have found that students with weak *visual processing* are more likely to have errors under categories 1, 2 and 3 and students with weak *auditory processing* are more likely to have a large number of errors under category 4.

Analysing errors and matching the learning strategy

A student with visual processing difficulties

Error analysis of the piece on p. 28 indicates that the vast majority of errors this student makes are in categories 1 or 3. (In some cases it is difficult to know whether the student doesn't know a convention of English or is confused by vowel sounds.) Such errors as 'injoy' for 'enjoy', 'cerface' for 'surface', 'whiserling' for 'whistling' indicate that this student has a good sense of the sounds of words but has poor visualising abilities.

His overdependence on sounds has led him to grammatical confusion (for example, 'regand' for 'regained', 'bin' for 'been'). Nonetheless, his apparently adequate auditory abilities indicate that learning strategies should build on this strength.

A student with visual processing difficulties would commonly have problems:

- visualising words: remembering the look of the word. Significant problems with doubling letters and homophones are often evident;

- recalling the letter sequence correctly (especially in non-phonetic words or word patterns);

- reversing or rotating letters (especially b/d but often p/g/q and sometimes w/m, n/u). Students will often use capital letters (B/D) in their writing to help reduce this confusion.

Late one night my friend woke me saying would you enjoy a trill run in my new helicopter i had secesly Scrambled in to my track suit Before we were away the lights of the City Clowed benith the stairs above i was begining to wonder aboat our destination when i calt Sight of the spinning Knife edge of the cenrace wat must of bin i tipe of flying Saser whiserling around us we doged scilfuly to avoyed an accident to our relife the space Craft regand hight and we Sank down to earth and the comflable bed i had never actily left.

The student with weak visual processing will often have adequate auditory sequencing and so can phonetically attack unlearned words. Thus this student's spellings often appear 'not bad' or in the category of 'good' guesses. Their attempts are often phonetically regular and thus readable or decipherable for the teacher. See Chapter 7, paying special attention to *auditory* approaches. Additional strategies which may be helpful include:

Writing words in segments or learning them rhythmically
Words are divided into small letter segments and the student says the letter names in rhythmic order. In effect, the student is letter-spelling as he or she writes. As this method is time consuming and slow, it is only recommended when sequencing problems are stubborn or the student cannot seem to visualise the spelling.

Example: The spelling word to be learned is 'special'. The student writes the word and chants the grouped letters as he or she writes: 'sp/ ec/ ia/ l'

The emphasis is on the rhythm of the groupings so that auditory skills can be used.

Making up mnemonics for segments of words
In this method, real words are substituted for the letters to help the student remember the order of letters. Students with sequencing problems (especially in relation to silent letters) may use this approach with some success. This method is also time-consuming and slow, but for some words this approach may be the only way to recall letter order.

Example: One student was learning the word 'bought'. She was having great difficulty remembering the order of the letters g,h,t. So she devised the mnemonic '*George Has Tea*' to remember the sequence. Whenever she came to that part of the word containing those three letters, she would recall 'George Has Tea' to remember the order.

The mnemonic needs to be developed *by the student*, otherwise it will not be a useful memory device.

A student with auditory processing difficulties

Error analysis of this student's work (see opposite) indicates that a large number of errors fall into category 4. This student is relying heavily on her visualising sense to recall words. Her auditory sense is so weak that she can only recall and sequence parts of many words. Visual learning strategies will be most helpful for this student.

Students with auditory perceptual problems often have *severe* spelling difficulties. This can occur even in students who are advanced readers. Their sense of the structure of some words may be very weak.

A student with auditory processing difficulties would commonly have problems:

● segmenting or sequencing sounds (for example, sounding out words or recalling sounds in order);

● 'holding' the sound in his or her head while writing it;

Lecut one night my friend waiok me saying would you injoy a trill run in my new hecotre. I had sarcley srambled into my track suit before we were away. The light of the city glowed beneth the staces abothe. I was begening to wonder about our desclernation when I cort siet of the spining kight kiee ega of the surpace of what must have been a type of flying sure willering around us to out relkie the space crapt regained hight and we sane down to eath and the counterde bad I had never acculiy left.

• checking a spelling phonetically.

This student is likely to use a visual approach to learning. Because he or she must rely *entirely* on this system, the spelling attempts may be missequenced and disordered.

We do not believe that remediating auditory processing disorders by drilling in sounds is a helpful approach for adults or adolescents. By the time a student is 10 or 11 years old, we feel his or her learning systems are so confused auditorally that unless the sound is easily recalled, spellings must be learned visually. Certainly, our experience is that phonic approaches are not often helpful in such cases.

Initially, the learner may need help in understanding what visualisation is. The Look, Cover, Write, Check Method is a good beginning *because it emphasises visualisation.*

See Chapter 7, paying special attention to the *visual* approaches such as: words-within-words, using coloured markers to emphasise parts of words, visually reorganising words.

Discussing the error analysis

Once an error analysis is complete, tutors and students are more likely to understand why a student continues to make a particular error even though he or she has spent time attempting to learn the spelling.

Throughout the teaching process the teacher must make time to discuss the spelling programme with the student, why and how errors are made, and then link appropriate learning strategies to new words. We have found it is helpful to stress the following points:

1 *Explain why the spelling is incorrect*
Unlike some students who can just learn the accurate version of a spelling by being corrected, students with specific difficulties will not remember a corrected spelling unless they understand what went wrong in their attempt. If an invented spelling is compared with the accurate spelling, some students cannot explain why they guessed what they guessed. On the other hand, if a student with auditory processing difficulties has attempted 'secesly' for 'scarcely' we can see that he or she is attempting to use visual memory (albeit not totally accurately) to recall the letters in the word. The overall configuration or 'outline' of this error follows the accurate spelling:

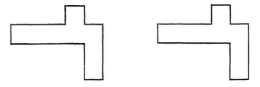

and many of the same letters occur in both words.

Thus because this student has difficulties sequencing sounds, he or she cannot check the spelling attempt through this system. Rather he or she can *only use a visual system.* In this light, this spelling attempt no longer looks 'stupid' to the student, but sensible because of the learning systems he or she can effectively access. If this student understands the error in this context, it is more likely that an accurate spelling will be remembered.

2 *Discuss the relationship of the error to the student's particular learning difficulty*
Students can be relieved of the guilt and embarrassment at forgetting a word or having difficulty learning it if they understand the relationship to their

own particular learning problems. Often, learners are frustrated at their problems in learning what appear to be 'simple' words. When examined further, many so-called 'simple' words are actually the most difficult to memorise because they have so little meaning (for example, 'the', 'does'). Or they don't follow English regularities and must be totally sight memorised ('yacht', 'friend'). Or they are homonyms and must be learned and recalled in a certain context.

If the student has innate visual weaknesses and sequencing problems, these kinds of errors are more likely to happen. Teachers should explain that problems in learning will undoubtedly occur *because of the learning difficulty*. For example, Alice was an adult student with auditory perceptual difficulties who had problems discriminating and segmenting sounds. Therefore, she often missequenced words or omitted significant sounds. Alice might spell 'scare' as 'sare' because she could not 'hear' the 'sc' blend. Once Alice understood she was likely to make this error (and no amount of training was likely to help her 'hear' the 'sc' blend), she felt easier about coming up with alternative methods for learning words and less frustrated about having difficulty learning them. Thus she learned the word as 's/care' because she knew the word 'care'.

3 *Explain why certain words are harder to learn*
Students must understand that if the spelling attempt or invention (i.e. the first guess) is visually and auditorally far from how a word is spelled, then this word will be difficult to learn. For example, if Jim spells 'frightened' as 'f r t d', a number of major structures have been omitted. Jim will have to do significant visualising work to remember this new word. It may take several weeks of practice. He should be aware that this word may take longer to learn than spelling attempts such as:

cair	*for*	care
chanse	*for*	chance
cerfice	*for*	surface

These spelling attempts follow both English spelling possibilities and also are visually/structurally similar. The more accurate the spelling when first attempted, the easier the word will be for the student to learn.

4 *Explain why student and teacher must mutually explore new ways of learning words*
Most students with specific or unique learning patterns have been *ineffectively* using spelling and learning approaches. Because no two people learn in exactly the same way, teachers and tutors can offer

methods which appear to be of the most value (and most successful), but students need to be involved in the identification process of selecting learning strategies.

For example, the student wants to learn to spell 'accommodate'. Several *visual* versions are offered to him or her:

acc	ommo	date	
ac	com	mod	ate

The student then selects the version which strikes him or her as the easiest to remember. He or she will then be expected to memorise it in this fashion. Because the student has selected the version and understands why it appeals, he or she will be more likely to remember the new spelling.

Activity 10.1   Identifying Specific Learning Difficulties

If you suspect that your student has specific learning difficulties, you could use the following questions in order to assess what line of action may be appropriate.

1 Does your student show significant discrepancy between verbal and written performance?

2 Does your student experience persistent or severe problems with spelling, even with 'easy' or common words?

3 Does your student:
  a easily lose his or her place when reading;
  b easily misread or miscopy;
  c experience left/right confusions;
  d have trouble 'seeing' his or her errors, even when these are pointed out?

4 Does your student exhibit memorising difficulties in other learning tasks, for example, lists, telephone numbers, data, names and dates?

5 Does your student have persistent problems with sentence structure, punctuation, and organisation of written work *not due* to lack of experience?

6 Does your student have trouble ordering things sequentially?

7 Does your student have trouble generalising, or acquiring and applying rules, although he or she may understand the principles of the rules?

8 Does your student have handwriting difficulties, 'messy' or poorly constructed handwriting?

9 Does your student have 'bad' days when he or she seems to be unable to remember words he or she already knew on a 'good' day?

Activity 10.2 **Error Analysis**

Error analysis chart

Using the following chart, classify your student's errors. See pp. 26–30 for a detailed discussion of error analysis.

Explanation of the columns:

1 Logical phonetic alternatives: 'hart' for 'heart'.

2 Visual sequencing error. 'dose' for 'does', 'flim' for 'film'.
3 Rule oriented errors: 'jock' for 'joke'.
4 Auditory perceptual errors: 'sramble' for 'scramble'.
5 Motor integration problems: 'rember' or 'rememember' for 'remember'.

It should be noted that column 1 errors are easier to rectify than those in other columns. Students with many errors in 3, 4, and 5 will take longer to learn these words and will need to try more strategies in order to learn them.

Correct Spelling (write in samples of each)	Spelling Attempt	1	2	3	4	5

Using Individualised Spelling Programmes with a Class

For the classroom teacher, the idea of teaching individualised spelling programmes may seem impractical, if not completely unrealistic. However, there are a number of ways of making such a scheme feasible and it is important to remember that even if it is more effort for the teacher, it is extremely effective for even the poorest spellers. Students' spelling, their interest in words, their writing and confidence all improve. Their interest in, and understanding of, their own learning often spills over into other areas of their schoolwork.

Initially, you may need considerable time to explain the spelling method to the students and to set up the programme. However, this can largely be done within the classroom framework as already suggested. Once students understand the method, many students (especially those with no particular spelling difficulties) will be able to work independently in selecting, grouping and devising ways of remembering words, as well as practising them over a prescribed period of time.

Shared words

Students studying the same subject, (for example, history, geography, biology) will often have a number of words in common which they are using in their writing. Such words will be a shared component of their individual spelling lists and can be a starting point for discussing strategies for remembering spellings. An example of such a discussion is given on Resource Sheet 12.

Students can work well in pairs on several aspects of a spelling programme:

1 They can experiment together with different ways of breaking up words. (See Chapter 7.)

2 They can test each other on the words they have been practising.

3 They can make up their own sentences each week on the words they got right and swap these sentences to dictate back to each other the following week.

4 They can check each other's lists to make sure words are accurately copied. This gives them extra practice in proofreading. We all know it is easier to spot someone else's errors than our own!

In this situation, the teacher can act as an adviser. Alternatively, he or she can work with one or two small groups who need more help while the others work independently, either on their spellings or on some other activity.

Selecting words

The selection of words for the weekly list can be done as part of the marking process, particularly on the rough draft. Instead of merely correcting spellings, the teacher can suggest spellings for the list and group these (as discussed in Chapter 6). It is helpful, however, to leave some choice for students if their motivation is to remain high.

It is also useful to encourage students to keep their own list of words they want to learn. This should be made up from

● words they feel unsure about spelling;
● words they have to look up in the dictionary or ask someone how to spell;
● words they continually get wrong;
● words that the teacher has picked out of their writing and suggested they learn;
● words they may need for a course or examination.

Students who need extra help

Admittedly, students with persistent spelling difficulties (see Chapter 10) will need more help in selecting words, breaking them up to facilitate learning, and following the method accurately. However, once the rest of the students are confidently embarked on their own spelling programme, it is possible to explore ways of giving more individual attention to those who need it.

Finally, the most important points to remember in developing individual tuition within a class are:

1 The need for *flexibility* in relation to the individual needs of the students within the class. This may require rethinking the purpose of class activities. It is more effective for students to spend 15–20 minutes working on tasks related to their specific needs than to spend one or two hours in activities which leave these needs unmet. As one student said poignantly, 'Every

year I would think, "This year it will be different" as I opened a clean new writing book. And every year my hopes collapsed: I still couldn't spell.' Yet no one ever helped her with her spelling.

2 The *responsibility* and *participation* of the students should be encouraged. Once a system of working in small groups and pairs is established, only minimal supervision is necessary. Students need to develop a sense of responsibility for and control over their own work. Teachers often need to be *facilitators* as much as they need to be teachers.

3 Working with a class does not necessarily mean that everyone has to do the same thing. It can rather be seen as a starting point from which individual students and small groups can develop in various ways and at different levels.

12

Follow-up: Why isn't Your Student Learning?

It is essential for the confidence of both the student and the teacher that spellings are learned successfully. If the student is not learning them, it is very important to find out why.

Often the student is not following the method correctly. Students need to understand the *reasons* for each step of the method. Frequently they do not realise the importance of following all the steps, have their own ideas about how to learn spellings (even if they don't work), or misunderstand instructions.

The most common reasons for not learning are failure in:

1 Covering Students may not be adequately covering the word before writing it. They may be peeping at the word as they·write it. By using visual cues they fail to get practice in retaining the image of the word.

2 Checking Students may not be checking back adequately, letter for letter. They may think they already know the word, or may just glance at it casually.

3 Visualising Students may put emphasis on testing themselves rather than on visualising or making an image. They may either try to memorise the whole list of words or get someone else to test them orally instead of *practising.*

4 Practising at prescribed intervals Students may forget to practise over the week and fill in all the columns of spellings just before the lesson.

It is also possible that students may be having specific difficulties which need to be worked on. Some possible problems for these students are:

● **Tracking** Students may be unable to keep track of sound sequences; they may telescope or lose parts of words, for example, 'avaible' for 'available' – or they may missequence parts of words, for example, 'orangisation' for 'organisation'. In this case, students need lots of practice with the teacher in breaking up words and saying the word in the corresponding 'bits' while writing it. It may help students to tap out the bits with their fingers as they say them. Such practice is especially important if the student is to handle polysyllabic words.

● **Proofreading** Students may miscopy or misspell words and have great difficulty seeing their errors. They need practice in checking the word back in segments with attention to the sequencing of letters.

● **Retaining spellings once learned** This generally indicates that the students are either not following the method accurately or need more practice and review. It is important to make sure that they are regularly producing writing in which they use the spellings they have learned. Students with severe difficulties need extra reinforcement and review.

If a student continues to find learning spellings particularly difficult after checking all the above possibilities, try using:

a plastic or magnetic letters. To reinforce letter patterns, take away initial letters and have the student replace them to make new words, for example, 'night', 'right', 'fight';

b the Fernald method of tracing words for motor reinforcement (see Bibliography).

c the Edith Norrie Letter Case (see Bibliography). This is a multi-sensory resource for students with specific learning difficulties.

13
Spelling and Handwriting

The importance of handwriting in learning to spell

The motor aspect of spelling is handwriting. When a writer prints, letters are isolated and the hand has no memory for how it feels to produce certain patterns of letters. By joining up letters, the chance of remembering a word is increased because the motor as well as the visual memory is being tapped. One student was being tested on her weekly spellings when she wrote one of her words 'without thinking – it just rolled off my pen', she said, amazed. This was her first experience of *automatic* spelling and writing.

If writing is to be fluent, both handwriting and spelling must be automatic, to allow attention to be given to the content and expression of what one is writing. It is therefore very important to encourage students to adopt a cursive style and to help them find a comfortable way to do this.

Some current research by Charles Cripps and Robin Cox, from The Cambridge School of Education (Cripps and Cox, 1989), indicates that young children taught connected script from the beginning (rather than taught to print first) not only develop fluent handwriting but also write longer pieces as well as becoming better spellers!

Many students continue to print because they have never been taught to join up their writing. A highly motivated student who has no physical disability can learn to write fluently in a matter of months. Other students continue to print because they have been told in the past that their joined-up writing was too messy. Although these students may need some help on developing fine motor control, they can usually develop a legible cursive script with help and practice.

Students with handwriting difficulties

If students cannot seem to control their pen, or print because their handwriting is messy or poorly constructed, they may be experiencing motor integration difficulties which interfere with developing a fluent script. For example, when forming letters they may have problems starting from the right point, changing direction in rotations and getting letters to 'meet up'. They may also reverse letters, for example, 'raddit' for 'rabbit'. Such students may also have difficulty keeping on the line and maintaining regular size and spacing.

Another handwriting problem may be perseveration (when the hand cannot stop repeating a pattern), for example, 'beginining' for 'beginning', 'openened' for 'opened'. Some students will say that their hand 'takes over' and, for instance, makes a 'd' when they mean to make a 'g'.

Although students with these problems may find it harder to acquire fluent and legible handwriting, they should be encouraged as the rewards in spelling, written expression and self-confidence are considerable.

Teaching handwriting

Often teachers are reluctant to teach handwriting because they feel it constricts students' development of their own handwriting style and constrains freedom and fluency of expressive writing. Much of this concern may be caused by the common approach to teaching handwriting through the copying of one particular style or another. Also, joined-up writing is often taught as if one must join *all* the letters; the emphasis is placed on not lifting the pen in the middle of a word. Understandably, such an approach may inhibit many students.

Consequently, it is important to approach cursive script through the actual motor experience of *how* we write. Understanding the basic movements involved in handwriting can help students develop a fluent handwriting style of their own.

Teachers often feel that repetitious exercises are monotonous and that students will find them boring. It is important that handwriting practice is limited to short, but frequent, 5–10 minute sessions. However, most students are very interested in their own handwriting (witness how many hours they may spend practising their signatures) and are eager to improve its quality.

How we write

There are two basic movements in handwriting: the arm moves the hand across the page and the fingers make the shapes of the letters. Sometimes students with handwriting difficulties do not understand these two movements; they may make the letters with the whole hand, which results in wobbly letters, or fail to move their hand across the page as they write and so get into a twist. Or they may fail to support the forearm so the letters are hard to control and the hand gets very tired.

Students also need to understand the way letter shapes are formed (no matter what the style); this involves rotation, rhythm and making strokes parallel. Emphasis should be on the development of kinaesthetic awareness through exercises to improve fine motor control and develop rhythmical movement patterns*

Ways to teach joined-up writing

Joining letters should be as natural as possible. Pointing out the ways different letters are linked can be useful for practice. However, we have found most success through encouraging students to join letters which they find easy to link, and then only two or three letters at a time at first. Joining letters can be effectively practised as part of the spelling programme so that, as words are learned, they are practised in cursive script.

Observe and discuss with students their current writing style. Students may need to experiment with different ways of holding the pen or positioning the paper; for instance, left-handed students may find it helpful to slant the paper to the right. Some students discover that their writing is difficult to control because they do not hold the paper with the non-writing hand; so their writing wobbles or they press hard to prevent the paper from sliding around.

It is also useful to explore options with students; there is more than one solution for writing letters which are difficult to join. For example *b* can become *b* , *r* can become *r* , *s* can become *s* . Alternatively, awkward letters may remain unjoined. Many students have given up cursive writing only because they could not manage to join two or three problem letters.

Trying a variety of writing implements can also make a difference. Many students use ball-point pens, for instance, which flow easily but also move easily in any direction on the surface of the paper, making them more difficult to control. Consequently, students may exert extra pressure and so tire themselves and slow their writing speed. A fountain or cartridge pen with a nib 'drags' more, so a change to one may facilitate handwriting. If students find nibbed pens difficult to use, they might also experiment with pencil or fine felt or fibre-tipped pens.

*We are indebted to Reginald C. Phillips in his book, The Skills of Handwriting, for these and other ideas and for the exercises on Resource Sheet 15.

Practical suggestions

It is often helpful to have a five minute 'warm-up' session before writing. Students can also do this at home, once or twice a day, especially if they have problems with handwriting. Such a session might include:

1 exercises to strengthen hand muscles, such as squeezing a rubber (squash) ball or manipulating clay or plasticine;

2 massaging fingers and hands to increase kinaesthetic awareness and release tension in hand muscles;

3 exercises to loosen up arm muscles to involve the whole arm, such as writing basic rhythmical movements (*uu mm eeee*) large on the blackboard, on newspaper pinned on the wall with thick crayons, or in the air. This tends to relax the hand and encourage a flowing movement;

4 practising basic movements and letter families (see Resource Sheet 15) on paper, starting small and getting bigger, then starting big and getting smaller;

5 experimenting with writing signatures.

Students may need specific instruction on where to start a letter and where to finish it. Exercises which demonstrate the construction of letters and how they are connected can be useful. It may be necessary to discuss in detail when construction problems are interfering with fluency (for example, when the student ends up in the wrong place for joining the next letter). Style may be awkward and messy at first, so encouragement to practise is needed until the production of letters is fluent and automatic.

It is helpful to get students to analyse their own handwriting. Most students are quick to tell you what they don't like about their handwriting. It is easier and more constructive to get students to identify and work on one or two things at a time and see an improvement than to try to change their handwriting completely.

General advice

● Some students have learned to hide spelling mistakes by making their handwriting, or certain words or letters, illegible. In such cases it is useful to discuss with them the importance of getting a clear image of a word in order to proofread and learn spellings; this is more difficult if spellings are disguised by handwriting.

Sometimes, working on spelling alone may improve handwriting. For instance, one student whose handwriting was very small and cramped with many indeterminate letters, began to write more clearly and in a larger script after only a few weeks of practising spellings; gaining confidence was all he needed.

● Lined paper (normal rather than fine width) should be used to encourage the development of an even, regular script. For students who have difficulty with ascending and descending letters as well as maintaining regularity of size, special handwriting paper or music paper may be helpful.

● If students consistently confuse, reverse or rotate certain letters or numbers, commonly b/d, p/q, m/w, z/s, 2/5, learning to join letters can help to reduce these confusions. The construction of each letter in connected script differs and the motor memory can reduce the visual memory confusions.

● If, after much practice, students continue to have severe handwriting problems, it may be especially important to help them to acquire keyboard skills and to have access to a word processor. For many students with motor integration and control difficulties, working on a keyboard enables them to make considerable leaps in developing written expression, as they are finally freed from having to give so much attention to the construction of letters.

14
Combining Spelling and Writing

It is a curious feature of our education system that, by the time children transfer . . . to secondary schools at eleven, the idea has become deeply ingrained that writing is an activity which requires you to dash down words on paper and then forget about them . . . . Writing has become for them a series of one-offs with little or no development between.
(from *Teaching Writing: The Development of Written Language Skills* by Geoffrey Thornton)

Spelling is a sub-skill of writing. This small but important point is often overlooked by teachers and students alike: in order to learn to spell you must write. Consequently students must write regularly as part of the spelling programme in order to:

a generate new spellings to learn;
b gain experience inventing spellings (which increases likelihood of learning spellings);
c consolidate spellings once learned.

It is extremely important that students understand this.

Editing and proofreading

Students are generally more willing to write without worrying about spelling and to risk inventing spellings if they understand the notion of a *rough draft* which is revised and corrected before writing a *final draft*. Introducing the processes of editing and proofreading enables students to see writing as something which can be developed and improved.

Who's the editor?

Many students assume that they write something once and are then finished with it; it is the teacher who does the correcting. Thus they feel that part of the teacher's job is to be their editor. The aspects of writing which includes transcription, for example spelling, punctuation and proofreading, belong to the teacher's domain.

Teachers may unwittingly fall victim to this misconception. In order to encourage students to develop composing skills (especially when stimulating reluctant writers), students may be told to ignore their mistakes so they do not worry too much about how their writing looks.

Other students may be so worried about making mistakes, that they write little and take no risks with vocabulary or trying to express complex ideas. They feel as if their writing is embossed in stone, unchangeable and there for eternity.

If, however, students are taught to see the first or rough draft as something they *themselves* correct and change, they become both less anxious and more in control of their own writing. Teachers can facilitate this by encouraging students to consider how they might improve their first drafts, for example, as far as expression, vocabulary and sentence structure are concerned. Students will often attempt a much richer vocabulary when they are not afraid of making mistakes and know they can learn the words they want to use. In addition, students learn to separate spelling from writing; this frees them to concentrate on what they are writing, with the confidence that they can learn the spellings later.

Activity 14.1   **Editing**

Purpose: To give students practice in editing so that they begin to become aware of writing as a process.

Use a piece of writing done by someone from another class so that students are not threatened by this activity. Have students work together in small groups to discuss the questions on Resource Sheet 16.

Correcting our own mistakes

Research in learning has shown that if we correct our own mistakes, rather than letting someone else correct them, we remember the correction more effectively. Thus if students participate in identifying and correcting their own spelling mistakes, they will remember the new spelling better than if the teacher returns a corrected copy. Merely correcting spellings *for* students generally has little effect, as every teacher who has painstakingly corrected the same spellings for a whole year will know!

Obviously, inexperienced writers will have less confidence as spellers and will thus need encouragment and help in developing proofreading skills. Other students who are especially weak spellers may have poor visual memories and experience difficulty in finding their errors. Nevertheless, with help, these students can improve their proofreading skills – while improving their written work as well.

Marking for meaning

Students often comment that teachers have been of little help when marking their work. Usually they recall red marks on a page and reminders, for instance, that their spelling is appalling.

There are times when students' work must be marked as a final version of an assignment. However, there should be other times when they are marked as part of the learning process and not just to estimate the value of the work. Students need models to learn from and a 'finished' piece of writing is perceived by students as just that: finished, of no further use. It is therefore not very easily learned from.

Students need help in the drafting and redrafting process. Initially, however, they should correct and revise the first draft themselves as much as possible. Only after the student has corrected and amended it should the teacher mark it. At this stage, marking should be aimed at helping students to check spellings, punctuation, grammar, etc. and to offer guidance on enriching vocabulary, when and how to expand an idea and where clarification is needed. It is important that suggestions made by the teacher are not just noted, but are *acted* upon by students in redrafting their work.

Errors in spellings that the student has already practised, sometimes spells correctly or has nearly right may be indicated by writing 'Sp' in the margin opposite the error. This encourages students to *find their own errors*. If the student still cannot 'see' the error, the teacher should underline the word.

Spellings which the student has not learned, but may wish to, should be written in the margin opposite the error. Students should then check their version against the correct one and write the correct one above the error; this allows students to 'take in' the correct spelling through writing it themselves.

If students make large numbers of errors, it is important to select only the ones they are most likely to be able to correct and learn, in order to give students the experience of success. It is much too discouraging to be faced with a margin crammed full of 'Sps' and corrected versions of misspelled words.

This error analysis marking can also be used for other types of errors (for example, 'P' for punctuation, 'SS' for sentence structure, etc.). It assists students in taking charge of their own learning through developing the skill of self-checking. Thus writing becomes a developmental *process* rather than a series of 'one-off' experiences.

Proofreading for errors

Often students do not really understand what proofreading means. When asked if they have proofread their work, they might justifiably say 'yes', but when the teacher reads it, the number of errors indicate that the student has not proofread for errors. Students often confuse reading for content (or what they wanted to say) with reading for error (or how they have presented it). Learners need to be shown *how* to read for content and *how* to read for error.

Some methods for proofreading include:

'Try to read your writing as if someone else has written it, to help you see the errors more easily.'

'Leave your writing until the next day, then re-read it and look for spelling mistakes.'

'Read your writing once for meaning and once for errors.'

'Read your writing aloud. This slows you down and helps you *hear* your errors.'

'Underline words you think are wrong and have someone else check to see if they are.'

Error analysis marking also helps students improve their proofreading skills.

Activity 14.2   Proofreading

Purpose: To encourage the development of self-checking skills.

Have students write a short piece during class time. Then have them answer the questions on Resource Sheet 17. The results of this activity should form the basis of a class discussion about proofreading.

Working with beginners

With students who are beginning writers, the spelling programme can still be used by building on *language experience* techniques. (For more information on language experience, see McFarlane, 1976 and Pratley, 1982.) In this case, students dictate to the teacher what they wish to write and the teacher acts as scribe, reading back what has been written and encouraging the student to make changes and expand where the student feels it is appropriate. (Thus editing can be done even when the student doesn't physically do the writing.) Spellings for the student to practise for the following week are then chosen from the piece of writing. Sentences based on these words are later dictated back to the student. Usually within a fairly short period of time, students will gain enough confidence to begin to write themselves, using invented spellings or even just guessing at the initial letters and getting the spellings from the teacher later.

It may be helpful with older beginners to focus the initial writing on one subject, for example, a hobby or topic of special interest, and to develop a large number of high usage words. This allows adequate reinforcement and practice and helps students master enough words on one subject to be able to write something meaningful fairly quickly. This increases motivation and confidence.

Encouraging and developing writing

• Avoid the use of dictionaries for spelling purposes. Students with spelling difficulties find using a dictionary frustrating and time-consuming when they do not know the likely alternatives for how a word might be spelled. This can discourage them from experimenting with words and inventing spellings.

• Have students write on loose A4 lined paper rather than in exercise books. This helps them develop the concepts of drafting and editing and the awareness that writing is a *process*.

• Encourage students to write on one side of the paper only. This makes it easier to see the continuity of their writing. It also makes it possible to cut up and rearrange or delete sections, which is a useful editing technique that can save much crossing out and rewriting.

The Benefits of Learning to Spell

Why Learn to Spell?

1 Your spelling will improve

You will learn to spell words you need to use in your writing every day. Although you may not become a perfect speller, your spelling will vastly improve and you will find it *useful*.

2 Your self-confidence as a writer will improve

Most students find that once they work on their spelling, they begin to take more risks in writing and see themselves as successful learners. Because you are remembering more words and using them regularly, you will feel more likely to succeed when learning other things.

3 Your fluency in writing will improve

Once your spelling improves you will find you can write automatically. There will be many words you no longer have to stop and think about. You will be able to think more about what you want to say rather than how to write it down on paper.

4 You will learn about why and how you make errors

In the process of learning to spell you will learn more about how and why English words are spelled the way they are. You will understand more clearly the value of 'guessing' at spellings in order to see what you do and do not know about the way words are built. In this way, you will be able to control your learning. You will choose which words you use, and they will have meaning for you.

5 You will find new ways to learn words and work out appropriate methods for the way you yourself learn.

Each person has a unique and personal learning style (the way in which you learn things). For many students, by focusing on spelling they can discuss their own learning style. Once this is done, you can use particular learning strategies to help you learn to spell better.

6 You will feel more in control of your writing

You will find you can enjoy writing and will feel less inhibited as a writer. The English language will be less difficult to understand, and you will find it less frustrating.

True/False Spelling Quiz

....   1 Reading a lot will help you with your spelling.

....   2 Learning to spell can help you with your reading.

....   3 Your handwriting is important when learning to spell.

....   4 When you are writing, you should stop at every word you cannot spell and look it up in a dictionary.

....   5 The sound of a word is a good guide to how you spell it.

....   6 Good spellers have a store of word pictures in their mind which they refer to when they want to spell a word.

....   7 If you look at a word long enough, you will learn how to spell it.

....   8 Writing a word helps you learn how to spell it.

....   9 Looking for words within a word can help you remember it.

....   10 Copying a word over and over is a good way to learn it.

A Hodder and Stoughton master

Finding the Rule

1 What rule can you make about adding suffixes (endings) to words from the following examples?

drop	dropped	dropping	dropper	
hug	hugged	hugging		
stop	stopped	stopping	stopper	
put		putting		
win		winning	winner	
stir	stirred	stirring		stirrup
hid	hidden			
red	redden		redder	reddest
sun	sunny			
mum	mummy			

2 What rule can you make about adding the suffix '-ing' to words from the following examples?

bake	baking	BUT	**see**	seeing
have	having		**flee**	fleeing
paste	pasting		**agree**	agreeing
bite	biting			
choose	choosing			
explode	exploding			
whistle	whistling			
trouble	troubling			
illuminate	illuminating			
recognise	recognising			

3 What rule can you make from the following examples?

all	always	**full**	hopeful
	also		careful
	almost		helpful
	altogether		grateful
	already		wonderful
	(Note: all right)		

4 What rule about adding the suffix '-ly' to words can you make
from the following examples?

deep-ly	BUT	**simple**	becomes	simply
wild-ly		**probable**		probably
brilliant-ly		**terrible**		terribly
love-ly		**possible**		possibly
immediate-ly		**visible**		visibly
sincere-ly				
absolute-ly				
final-ly				
social-ly				
general-ly				
practical-ly				
careful-ly				
awful-ly				
grateful-ly				
wonderful-ly				

5 What rule can you make about adding suffixes to words from
the following examples?

try	tries	tried		BUT	trying
cry	cries	cried			crying
fly	flies	flier			flying
copy	copies	copier			copying
bury	buries	burial			burying
deny	denies	denial			denying
marry	marries	marriage			marrying
happy	happier	happiness	happily		
pretty	prettier	prettiness	prettily		
lazy	lazier	laziness	lazily		
steady	steadier	steadiness	steadily		

ALSO **key**	keys			
day	days			
boy	boys			
stay	stays	stayed		staying
play	plays	played	player	playing
buy	buys		buyer	buying
employ	employs	employed	employer	employing
destroy	destroys	destroyed	destroyer	destroying

Figure (i)

THE DINNER BELL.

The hands on the clock gradually crept nearer and nearer to twelve o'clock. Eventuly the bell rang with it's usual deafning dinn. The sound of desks being slamed shut, chair legs being scraped on the stone floor, could be heard above the chatter of hungry little boy's and girls. As they made there way to the holl which doubled as the canteen. We all stood in a long line which stretched from the holl dawn the corridoor. The other part of the school were by now playing in the play ground. They would have there dinner later.

It was possible as I rember to tell the various day's of the week by the smells that emerged from the kitchen On Fridays the unmistakable smell of fish cakes with chips could be smelt. On Monday it was meat pie and peas.

Eventually we would reach the holl, where four or fine dinner ladies stood dressed entialy in whight. Thay stood behind a low shelf that was constantly wipped clean when in use. Large stanlas-steel trays were placed on the shelf, one tray for a diffrent food. As we wolke passed me would pick up a tray, two plates and a knife, fork and spoor Each dinner ladies would place a large portion of food onto your plate, with a tray of very hot food balanced precarisly on the tray, me wolked to a table.

A Hodder and Stoughton master

Figure (ii)

I dialed the first two numbers when I released that some one was speaking on the line. The voice souned formiler. It was Steela. I was so taking a back. that I was Dumb Sunk. I just stood thir and Listen.

"It's just that he dose undersand what its like to be stuck in here the house all the time. Having to depend on him for every thing. he seem to have forgot that before Tommy was born, I had a good Job, it was well payed. I thenk if I was somebody, not Just John's wipe. He wants me to fall in with his image of the little wipe at home wanting for hubby to come home or intaning his friends from the offices. And Know his up for promotions, and if he gets it, I'll be expected to acomping him like some pet dog folaing my Lord and Mastor.

"It's just that I wont to go back to work, when Tommy is a little more stent. Its not that I dont love them both. Its Just......

Steela began to Cry....

I wanted to say some thing but my Mout was Dry. I put down the receiver.

Figure (iii)

Descirbtion of Ian

Just has I truned The corner to Michelle road out of no where jumped Ian Jhonson (Pogo for short). he was the most disliked person in our school, he would alway look as if he heed splet in his uniform the night before and they were nother clean. His shirt which was suposed to be white was a sort of greyish colour. The arms were too small for him, his tourser was even worse, so black th didn't show the dity. They had holes where the knee shoul have been. His hair was alway a thick black mess which I don't supose every saw a comb. With a face lik a bull dog Pogo seam to fit him very well. The other boys were alway making fun of him but this did not seem to make much diffence. He was a patricual joker who would always be firtening someone with some thing.

" what on earth did you do that for ? "
With a grine form cheek to cheek he replied, " I knew you were comeing alone so wanted to suprise you. "
" Well you did a good job of that now get out of my way I have things to do. "
" not before I tell you the good news " he said,
" What good news could you possuble have for me:
" You never guess, " he said.
" No what is it ? "
" I'm talking you to the school dance, ", , ,

Spelling Histories

Previous spelling experience

- How would you rate yourself as a speller on a scale of 1–5?
  1 Excellent   4 Poor
  2 Good   5 Awful
  3 OK

- Why do you think you're a good/bad speller?

- What have teachers said about your spelling in the past?

- How have you been taught or not taught spelling in the past?

- Did you find these methods/approaches helpful?

- Have you ever felt embarrassed about your spelling or mistakes you have made?

Current spelling attitudes

- What do you think is the importance of good spelling?

- When you want to learn a word nowadays, how do you do it?

- Have you ever tried any method you know *didn't* work for you?

Identifying Your Learning Style

Given below are a number of incomplete sentences and three ways of completing each one. In each case, select the way which most frequently represents your personal preference. In each case make only ONE choice.

	A	B	C
1 When you keep up with currents events, do you:	read the newspaper thoroughly	listen to the radio and/or watch the TV news	quickly read the paper and/or spend a few minutes watching the TV news
2 When you dress, are you:	a neat dresser	a sensible dresser	a comfortable dresser
3 When you read novels, do you:	like descriptive scenes/stop to imagine the scene/take notice of pictures	enjoy dialogue and conversation/'hear' the characters talk	prefer action stories and are not a keen novel reader
4 When you spell, do you:	try to see the word	try to sound out the word	write the word down to find out if it 'feels' right
5 When you are angry, do you:	clam up, seethe, give others the 'silent' treatment	quickly let others know and express it in an outburst	storm off, clench your fists, grit your teeth or grasp something tightly
6 When you are free and have spare time, would you rather:	watch TV, go to the cinema/theatre or read	listen to records or the radio, go to a concert or play an instrument	do something physical, for example, sport, DIY
7 When you forget something, do you:	forget names but remember faces	forget faces but remember names	forget faces and names but remember what you did
8 When you have to discuss something important with another person do you:	prefer face-to-face meetings or writing letters	use the telephone	talk it out during another activity, for example, walking or having a meal
9 When you enjoy the arts, do you:	like paintings	like music	like dancing
10 When you are talking, do you:	talk sparingly, but dislike listening for too long	enjoy listening, but are impatient to talk	gesture a lot and use expressive movements
11 If you are going to a meeting or group discussion, do you:	come prepared with notes	enjoy discussing issues and hearing other points of view	wish to be somewhere else and spend the time doodling

A Hodder and Stoughton master

12	When you are with others, might they interpret your emotions from your:	facial expressions	voice quality	general body language
13	When you visualise, do you:	see vivid detail, see vivid pictures	think in sounds	have few images, but those that you do have involve movement
14	When you are concentrating, are you:	distracted by untidiness or movement	distracted by sound or noises	distracted by movement
15	When you are praised, do you:	like written comments	like spoken comments	like a physical action, such as a pat on the back or a hug
16	If you needed to discipline a child, would you:	temporarily isolate the child from others	reason with the child and discuss the situation	use 'acceptable' forms of corporal punishment, for example, a smack
17	When you try to interpret someone's mood, do you:	look primarily at their facial expressions	listen to their tone of voice	watch their body movements
18	When you are inactive, do you:	look around, doodle, watch something	talk to yourself or other people	fidget
19	When you are learning, do you:	like to see demonstrations, diagrams, slides, posters	like verbal instructions, talks and lectures	prefer direct involvement, for example, activities, role-playing
20	When you go on a new, long journey, do you:	get the route from a book, for example, AA/RAC guide	talk to someone to get the information	get out maps, etc. and make a plan

TOTAL

Now discuss the following questions:

1 Under which column did you tick the most answers?

2 What kind of a learning preference does it appear you have?

3 What learning methods seem to suit your style (for example, through lectures or demonstrations)?

4 What methods of learning will not be suited to your learning style (for example, through lectures, watching films, reading)?

5 Think of three methods you have observed teachers using. Do these methods suit your style? How?

6 How do most of the students in your class learn best?

This activity is reproduced courtesy of Peter Moule, Westminster College of Further Education.

Analysing Errors

Use the dictation below and the analysis chart on Resource Sheet 7b to help you analyse different errors.

> Leat one night my friend waok me saying would you injoy a trill run in my new hecotre? I had sarcley srambled into my trak suit before we were away. The lights of the city glowed beneath, the stars abothe. I was begening to wonder about our desdernation when I cort siet of the spining kife ege of the surface of what must have been a type of flying sorser wisterling around us. To our releaf the space craft regained hight and we sanc down to erth and the comftable bed I have never acherly left.

Put the spelling mistakes from the above dictation under the different categories on the analysis chart.

1 In which column are there the most errors?

2 Do you think this student has the most trouble:
a Remembering how words look?
b Remembering how words (or letters) sound?
c Missing out bits of words?

3 If this student should learn according to his or her learning styles, what kind of spelling strategies do you think he or she will need?

4 Now ask your teacher to dictate some text to you and analyse your own errors in the same way.

Analysing Errors

Analysis Chart

1 SPELL IT LIKE IT SOUNDS	2 DON'T KNOW RULE	3 GET LETTERS OUT OF ORDER	4 MIX UP SOUNDS	5 MISS OUT OR ADD BITS

Selecting Words to Learn

Go through a piece of your writing and underline any words you think you have misspelled. Find out the correct spellings from your teacher.

1 Are there any which have the same letter patterns?

like   str*ength*   w*ould*
                 length   or   c*ould*
                                           sh*ould*

or   st*ation*   capital*ism*
        inform*ation*   or   social*ism*
             *nation*al

If so, group them together.

2 Are there any words which have a root word in common?

like   sub *ject*   *('ject' is the Latin root for 'throw')*
         ob *ject* ion
         re *ject* ed

or   *appoint* ment
     dis *appoint* ed

If so, group them together.

3 Are there any which are similar to another word you already know?

like pr*oud* (if you already know *loud*)
or   sw*itch* (if you already know *itch* or k*itch*en)

If so, write the word you know next to the one you don't know to help yourself remember.

4 Are there any words you confuse like 'as' and 'has' or 'their' and 'there'?

If so, remember: *Don't try to learn them together; it will just confuse you more.* Instead, decide to learn only one of the confusing words at a time and link it with a word that will help you remember what it *means*.

For instance, link   *there*
           with   *here*
           and   *where*

They all have 'here' in them and they all refer to a place.

Another week, link   *their*
           with   *her*
           and   *his*

They all show that something belongs to someone (her hat, his hat, their hats).

Finally, are there any words you *need* to learn because you use them a lot or will need them for an examination? Are there any words you really *want* to learn because you want to be able to write them with confidence? Add a few of these words to your list. You should not have more than 10–15 words to learn in any one week.

    Make a list of words you want to learn and keep adding to it. Tick off the ones you have learned.

    Remember to use the words you have learned in your writing. The more you use them the more you can be sure you will not forget them!

A Hodder and Stoughton master

Memory

Characteristics of short-term and long-term memory

	Short-term memory (working memory)	**Long-term memory** (permanent memory)
Capacity	limited	practically unlimited
Persistence	very brief	practically unlimited
Access	immediate	depends on organisation
Input	very fast	relatively slow

(from Comprehension and Learning by F. Smith)

Points to remember:

1 The short-term memory can hold from five to nine items at one time. Some people can hold more in their short-term memory store than others. Most people can hold about seven items.

2 By 'chunking', or grouping items together, we can remember more items more easily. For instance, we remember phone numbers in groupings of three and four numbers. Most of us learned the alphabet in chunks:

    abcd   efg   hijk   lmnop   qrst   uvw   xyz
                      (seven groups)

Although most of us would have difficulty learning the sequence 'xoqtxaobhfmr', we could easily remember the nonsense word 'fortenmaster' (with the same number of letters) because we can chunk the letters together: for/ ten/ master. So we only have to remember three bits instead of twelve!

3 When retrieving items from long-term memory, there is a difference between RECOGNITION and RECALL. In reading we only have to *recognise* the words; in spelling we have to *recall* them, letter for letter and in the right order.

4 Memory is aided by *frequency, recency* and *value*. That is, we remember things best that we use or practise frequently, that we have learned recently, and that are important or meaningful to us.

5 How we organise information can affect how we retrieve it from the long-term memory. The way we structure, associate and link information gives us 'hooks' for retrieving it. Meaning, pattern, rhythm, images and reciting all help.

Memory and Spelling

Research on learning by psychologists has given us some useful information about how our memory works:

a We remember things more easily if we organise them into groups, patterns, categories.

b We remember unusual things.

c We remember things that interest us most.

d We can only remember a few things at a time (7, plus or minus 2 'chunks').

e It is difficult to remember things we don't understand.

f Our memory works by building links.

g We remember things better if we already know something about them.

h Learning is an active task – we have to think about *how* we can remember something.

After a period of learning, recall rises for a short while (about ten minutes) and then falls steeply (80 per cent of detail is forgotten after 24 hours).

However, with proper *review* after ten minutes, then within 24 hours, again within a week, and so on, recall can be maintained *long-term*. The following graph shows how properly spaced review can keep recall at a high level.

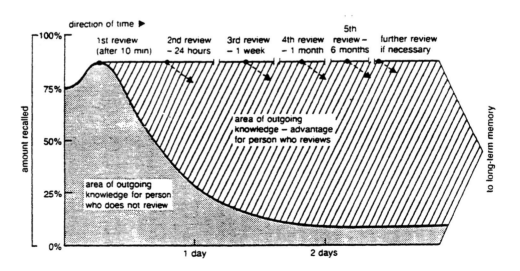

From Use Your Head New Revised Edition by Tony Buzan

Ways to Help Remember Spellings

1 *Beat out the syllables* and write out each 'bit' of a word as you say it.

2 *Highlight* the difficult bits of the word.

3 *Link* a new word with words you already know:

s*ound* – r*ound* – gr*ound*   r*ain* – tr*ain* – Brit*ain*

If you are a visual learner:

1 Change the *look* of the word:

div/ ide   div ide   d ⬛ivi⬛ de

re ce ive   r/ ece / ive   r ⬛ece⬛ ive

2 Find *words within words*:

fat her   cap a city

If you are an auditory learner:

1 Change the *sound* of the word
Exaggerate the pronunciation or 'say it funny':

be – ca – use   parli – *a* – ment

2 Say the names of the letters in *rhythm*:

p-e o-p l-e   q-u e-u e

especially confusing *endings*: -t-i-o-n   -g-h-t   -c-i-a-l

If you are a kinaesthetic or physical learner:

Trace the letters with your forefinger as you say or visualise the word.

For everyone:

1 Learn the *derivations* of words:

> television: 'tele' means afar, over a distance
> 'visio' means sight (from Latin)

2 Remove or add *prefixes* and *suffixes*:

> *un*-like-*ly*   *in*-vis-*ible*   *un*-*re*-strict-*ed*

If you're really stuck:

Make up a *mnemonic* (from the Greek root for 'remember'). A menmonic is a verse, rhyme or other device to aid the memory, for example, 'Never be*lie*ve a *lie*; 'Big Elephants Aren't Ugly, they are BEAUtiful!

Students Talking About Spelling

Part of the spelling programme involves talking about each word, discussing how to remember it and deciding where to break it up in order to learn it most easily. Susan, Veronica, Steve, Richard and John are on an intensive short course at college and have words in common that they need to learn.

The following are excerpts from their discussions of how to learn their words.

property

Steve: 'Oh, it's got 'rope' in it: p/ *rope/* r/ ty.'
John: 'I couldn't learn it like that. I've got to have it the way it sounds: prop/ er/ ty.'

registration

Steve: 'I can remember it because it's got a "rat" in it: regist/ *rat/ ion.*'
Richard: No, I do it: reg is tra tion. I'm an expert on breaking down words now. It's pissing easy, learning spellings like this.'

casualty

Richard: 'I do it how it sounds: [says] cas *you* al ty, [writes] cas/ u/ al/ ty.'
Veronica: 'It's less confusing to write it down like this: cas u al ty – because the spaces between the letters make it look clearer.'

equipment

Tutor: '"Q" is always followed by "U", like in "equipment" or "quiet". That's a rule, though I suppose there might be an exception.'
Steve: 'Like GATQWICK!'
Richard: (good humouredly) 'No, you berk! That's just an advertisement.'
  [Everyone, including Steve, laughs.]
Tutor: 'That proves that a lot of spelling is remembering how a word looks. You've probably been on a bus staring at that poster and the word has stuck in your mind.'

quiet

Veronica: 'I get "quite" and "quiet" mixed up. Oh! I know – I could say "ET is qui-et". Then I'd remember it was -et.'

facilities

Tutor: How do you remember this one?'
Veronica: 'I don't think of the sounds. I do it fac ili ties. I remember it's got three 'i's and then I check to see if it looks right.'
Susan [practising]: 'I never thought I could learn spellings like this [using the Look, Cover, Write, Check Method]. When anyone used to ask me how to spell something, I'd tell them to look it up! Now if it's something we've done, like "immediately", I tell them straightaway. Me and Steve, we've been practising our words, and during the day we'll call out a word to each other and shout out the spelling back.'

We would like to thank Liz Fannin and her students at Brixton College for this dialogue.

Word Building

When learning to spell it helps to know the structure of a word.

The structure of a word is the way it is put together: **prefix + root + suffix**.

Here are some examples of how words are structured in this way:

Latin root: ject (throw)

de	ject	ed	(de: down, away from)
de	ject	ion	
re	ject		(re: again, back)
ob	ject		(ob: against)
ob	ject	ive	
sub	ject		(sub: under)
sub	ject	ive	
in	ject	ion	(in: in, into)
ad	ject	ive	(ad: to, towards)
pro	ject	ion	(pro: before, for)

Latin root: soci (unite)

	soci	al	
a	soci	al	(a/ab: from away)
	soci	ety	
as	soci	ate	(ad: to, towards – note that the 'd' in 'ad' becomes an 's' to make pronunciation easier)
dis	soci	ate	(dis: apart, away)

Greek root: pathos (feeling)

a	path	y	(a/ab: without)
sym	path	y	(sym/syn: with)
sym	path	etic	
em	path	y	(em: put into, bring into)
tele	path	ic	(tele: from afar)

Old Norse (Viking) root: taka (take)

mis	take		(mis: wrong/bad)
over	tak	en	
under	tak	er	
par	tak	ing	

(See Signposts to Spelling by Joy Pollock for more examples.)

The Look, Cover, Write, Check Method

Use an exercise book to put your spellings in. Divide each page of a double page spread into two columns so that you have four columns across the pages (see example below), and number the columns. Select with your teacher which words you will learn and find the best way for *you* to remember each word.

Write each word in column 1 and have your teacher make sure you have copied them correctly. Then practise each word, *one at a time*, in the following way:

1 LOOK at the word, noting which bits are especially difficult, and *say* the word aloud. Close your eyes and try to 'see' it.

2 COVER the word and remind yourself how you will remember it.

3 WRITE the word in column 2. Say it as you write it. If you have learned it in bits, say each bit as you write it.

4 CHECK the word, letter for letter, to see if you have written it correctly. If you have not, put an X next to the wrong spelling and copy the correct spelling above or near it. Pay attention to your mistake. Don't just stick in a missing letter, but write out the *whole word* correctly to help your hand remember it the next time.

5 One day later, repeat the process and write the word in column 3.

6 Two or three days later, repeat the process and write the word in column 4.

Remember: you are *practising* the words, not testing yourself yet.

1.	2.	3.	4.
Shake	Shake	Shake	Shackee X / Shake
Shaking	Shaking	Shaking	Shaking
taking	taking	taking	taking
allow	allow	allow	allow
Coward	Coward	coward	Coward
Particular	particular	particular	particular
Particularly	Particularly	Particularly	Particular
article	article	articual X / article	Article
rainy	rainy	Rainy	rainy
wait	Wait	wait	wait
await	await	await	await
awaiting	awaiting	awaiting	awaiting

7 A week after you have first practised them, get your teacher or another student to test you on the words you have learned.

8 Then, on a separate piece of paper, make up sentences using the words you have learned and get your teacher or another student to dictate them to you a week later. This will help you check that you have got the words into your long-term memory.

If you have mispelled any words, put them onto your *new* list so that you can practise them again. Remember that it may take longer to learn some words, especially ones you have been spelling incorrectly for a long time.

A Hodder and Stoughton master

How We Write

In order to write fluently across the page we need to make two separate movements.

First, our arm and hand must move across the page from left to right.

Second, our fingers must move to make the letters.

1 Make sure your writing arm is supported. (Put your weight on the opposite hand or arm.) Holding your pen, move your arm and hand across the page without moving your fingers.

2 Now, move your fingers while keeping your hand and arm still.

These are the two basic parts of handwriting: the arm moves the hand across the page and the fingers make the shapes of the letters.

3 Now, just move your fingers at first, then begin to move your arm across the page slowly continuing:

Make your arm move faster:

Make your hand move more slowly:

4 Practise these patterns to strengthen your finger movement and control. Try to feel your hand and fingers working together.

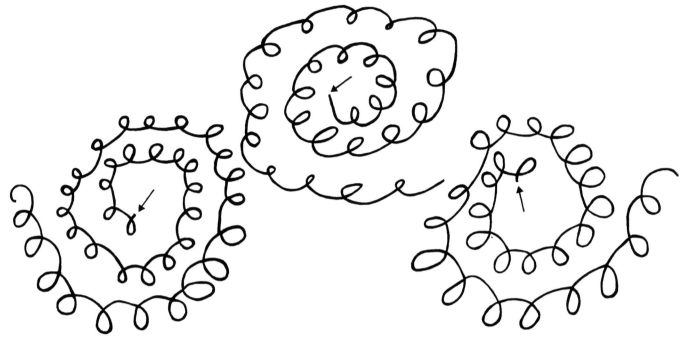

5 The downward movement is the most important handwriting stroke. Try to make the downstrokes parallel and at regular intervals.

NOT

Practise making short strokes onto a single line, trying to maintain a downward rhythm.

They should look like this:

If you have trouble doing this, do not forget to move your arm after every few strokes.

6 We also have to change directions when we make letters:

Practise letter families for difficult letters:

Or practise them in groups of three:

Editing

Read the piece of writing handed to you by your teacher and discuss the following questions. Someone in each group should make notes.

1 What did you like about it?

2 What questions would you like to ask the writer? Do these tell you where you feel the writer could expand or say more?

3 Were there any bits in the piece that you didn't understand? Do these tell you where the writer needs to be clearer?

4 Were there any problems that interfered with your reading of the piece, for instance, spelling or punctuation?

5 Where could the writer have used more interesting or exact words? 'Nice', for instance, is rather vague.

As a class, share what the groups thought about the above questions and use them for a general discussion about editing.

Now look at a piece of your own writing and ask yourself the same questions. Redraft your piece of writing and see how much you can improve it.

Proofreading

1 Read your piece of writing through twice. Try to read it as if it were written by someone else.

  a On the *first* reading, read for *content*:
  - does it make sense?
  - does it say what you intend to say?
  - are there any bits you need to improve?

  b On the *second* reading, check *punctuation*, *grammar* and *spelling*.

2 Leave your piece of writing until the next day. Now read it again. Can you find more mistakes this time? Do you feel differently about what you wrote? If so, why do you think this is?

3 *Underline* the spellings you think are wrong.

  a If you think you can correct any, write the correct spelling above the error or in the margin.

  b Ask your teacher for the correct spellings of the words you don't know. Select some to learn for next week, using the Look, Cover, Write, Check Method.

4 *If you would like to*, exchange your piece of writing with that of a classmate and proofread each other's work. Did you find more errors? Do you think it is easier to proofread someone else's writing than your own? Why?

Bibliography

Spelling

ALBSU (1988) *The Spelling Pack*, Adult Literacy and Basic Skills Unit, Kingsbourne House, High Holborn, London.
Allan, B. V. (1977) *Logical Spelling*, Collins.
Brown, H. and Brown, M. (1987) *A Speller's Companion*, Brown and Brown.
Cripps, C. (1978) *Catchwords. Ideas for Teaching Spelling*, Harcourt Brace Jovanovich, Sydney.
Fernald, G. M. (1943) *Remedial Techniques in Basic School Subjects*, McGraw-Hill.
Frith, U. (1980) *Cognitive Processes in Spelling*, Academic Press, 1980.
Hornsby, B. and Shear, F. (1980) *Alpha to Omega*, Heinemann.
Moorhouse, C. (1977) *Helping Adults to Spell*, Adult Literacy and Basic Skills Unit, as above.
Peters, M. (1970) *Success in Spelling*, Cambridge Institute of Education.
Peters, M. (1975) *Diagnostic and Remedial Spelling Manuel*, Macmillan Education.
Peters, M. (1985) *Spelling: Caught or Taught: A New Look?*, Routledge and Kegan Paul.
Pollock, J. (1978) *Signposts to Spelling*, Heinemann Educational Books.
Temple, C. A., Nathan, R. G. and Burris, N. A. (1982) *The Beginnings of Writing*, Allyn and Bacon, Inc.
Temple, M. (1978) *Get it Right*, John Murray.
Todd, J. (1982) *Learning to Spell: A Resource Book for Teachers*, Basil Blackwell.

On video
BBC Spelling Series (1988) *Spell it Out*, BBC Publications.
ILEA (1986) *Teaching Adult Literacy, Unit B: Strategies for Teaching Spelling*, Centre for Learning Resources, 275 Kennington Lane, London SE11 5QZ.

Memory and learning

Ansell, G. (1984) *Make the Most of Your Memory*, National Extension College.
Baddeley, A. (1982) *Your Memory: A User's Guide*, Penguin Books.
Buzan, T. (1974) *Use Your Head*, BBC Publications.
Gregorc, A. F. (1979) 'Learning/teaching styles: Potent forces behind them', *Educational Leadership*, pp. 234–236.
Gregorc, A. F. (1979) 'Learning/teaching styles: Their nature and effects' in *Student Learning Styles: Diagnosing and Prescribing Programs*, NASSP, Reston, VA.
Gregorc, A. F. (1982) 'Learning style/brain research: Harbinger of an emerging psychology' in *Student Learning Styles and Brain Behavior*, NASSP, Reston, VA.
Smith, F. (1975) *Comprehension and Learning*, Holt, Rinehart and Winston.

Reading and the psycholinguistics of reading

Arnold, H. (1982) *Listening to Children Reading*, Hodder and Stoughton.
Smith, F. (1978) *Reading*, Cambridge University Press.
Clay, M. (1979) *Reading, The Patterning of Complex Behaviour*, Heinemann.
McFarlane, T. (1976) *Teaching Adults to Read*, Macmillan.
Pratley, R. (1982) 'The Language Experience Approach to Literacy Teaching', ALBSU Newsletter insert.

Specific learning difficulties

Ellis, A. (1984), *Reading, Writing and Dyslexia: A Cognitive Analysis*, Lawrence Erlbaum Associates.
Farnham-Diggory, S. (1978) *Learning Disabilities*, Fontana.
Hornsby, B. (1984) *Overcoming Dyslexia*, Martin Dunitz.
Jordan, D. R. (1972) *Dyslexia in the Classroom*, Charles E. Merrill.
Jorm, A. F. (1983) *The Psychology of Reading and Spelling Difficulties*, Routledge and Kegan Paul.
Simpson, E. (1981) *Reversals*, Gollancz.
Snowling, M. (ed.) (1985) *Children's Written Language Difficulties*, NFER/Nelson.
Springer, S. and Deutsch, G. (1981) *Left Brain, Right Brain*, Freeman and Co.
Thomson, M. (1984) *Developmental Dyslexia*, Edward Arnold.
The Edith Norrie Letter Case, obtainable from the Helen Arkell Dyslexia Centre, Frensham, Farnham, Surrey.

Dyslexia Series:
A Dyslexic's Eye View
The Problem of Spelling
The Problem of Reading
The Problem of Sequencing and Orientation
The Problem of Handwriting
Motivation
Speech Therapy and the Dyslexic
Numeracy
Published and obtainable from the Helen Arkell Dyslexia Centre, Frensham, Farnham, Surrey.

Handwriting

Barnard, T. *Handwriting Activities*, Ward Lock Education Basic Skills Series.
Boult, T. and Douglas, T. (1985) *Improve Your Handwriting*, Edward Arnold.
Cripps, C. and Cox, R. (1989) *Joining the ABC*, Learning Developing Aids.
Jarman, C. (1982) *The Development of Handwriting Skills*, Basil Blackwell.
Phillips, R. C. (1976) *The Skills of Handwriting*, R. C. Philips Ltd.
Ridgeway, B. (1981) *Setting Out Word-Bank and Handwriting*, Edward Arnold.
Sassoon, R. (1983) *The Practical Guide to Children's Handwriting*, Thames & Hudson.
Sassoon, R. and Briem, G. S. E. (1985) *Teach Yourself Handwriting*, Hodder and Stoughton.
Taylor, J. *Writing is for Reading*, available from 14 Dora Road, London SW19.
Waller, E. (1978) *Dyslexia: The Problem of Handwriting*, Helen Arkell Dyslexia Centre, Frensham, Farnham, Surrey.

Teaching writing

Atwell, N. (1987) *In the Middle: Writing, Reading and Learning with Adolescents*, Heinemann, New Jersey.
Clay, M. (1975) *What Did I Write?*, Heinemann.
Elbow, P. (1976) *Writing Without Teachers*, Oxford University Press.
Gardner, S. (1985) *Conversations with Strangers*, Adult Literacy and Basic Skills Unit, as above.
Graves, D. H. (1984) *Writing: Teachers and Children at Work*, Heinemann, New Jersey.
Mace, J. (1980) *Learning from Experience*, Adult Literacy Support Services Fund.
Shaughnessy, M. P. (1977) *Errors and Expectations*, Oxford University Press, New York.
Smith, F. (1982) *Writing and the Writer*, Heinemann.
Swinney, J. *Stimulating Writing: Wages to Windscale*, Friends Centre, Brighton.
Temple C. A. *et al.*, op. cit.
Thornton, G. (1980) *Teaching Writing: The Development of Written Language Skills*, Edward Arnold.